the SUSTAINABLE BUSINESS CHALLENGE

A briefing for tomorrow's business leaders

Jan-Olaf Willums

with the World Business Council for Sustainable Development

A global initiative by the Foundation for Business and Sustainable Development
in collaboration with the United Nations Environment Programme
and the Bellagio Forum for Sustainable Development

**Foundation for Business
and Sustainable Development**

Greenleaf **Publishing**

1998

For the *Sustainable Business Challenge Exam*, log in at
http://www.wbcsd.ch/foundation/

The Sustainable Business Challenge was produced with the input from business people and experts from environmental and academic organisations. It therefore aims to reflect many *different views* on sustainable development, underscoring the Foundation's and WBCSD's wish to be partners for dialogue with other groups. This means that not every contributing partner in this project will necessarily agree with every word.

This work, although intended to be of an educational nature, contains fictitious characters and organisations. In particular, 'SDX Corporation', *International Business Issues*, 'The Green Business Network', *International Marketing, Forward*, 'The Intergovernmental Panel on Industry' and 'Environics' are purely fictitious creations as are the characters who are described as working for them. Any resemblance to any actual organisation or business or any person living or dead is purely coincidental.

© 1998 The Foundation for Business and Sustainable Development

Published by Greenleaf Publishing and The Foundation for Business and Sustainable Development
Greenleaf Publishing is an imprint of
Interleaf Productions Limited
Broom Hall
Sheffield S10 2DR
England

Typeset by Interleaf Productions Limited and printed in Singapore on environmentally friendly, acid-free paper from managed forests.

British Library Cataloguing in Publication Data:

Willums, Jan-Olaf
    The sustainable business challenge : a briefing for
    tomorrow's business leaders. - (Foundation for business and
    sustainable development)
    1. Environmental policy   2. Social responsibility of business
    3. Environmental management
    I. Title   II. World Business Council for Sustainable
    Development   III. United Nations Environment Programme
    IV. Bellagio Forum
    658.4'08

ISBN 1874719179

Images © 1997 PhotoDisc, Inc.

**World Business Council
for Sustainable Development**

The WBCSD is a coalition of over 120 international companies united by a shared commitment to the environment and to the principles of economic growth and sustainable development. Its members are drawn from 35 countries and more than 20 major industrial sectors. The WBCSD also benefits from a global network of 15 national business councils, as well as regional business councils and partner organisations in developing countries and economies in transition. Its objectives are:

Business leadership — to be the leading business advocate on issues connected with the environment and sustainable development

Policy development — to help create a framework that allows business to contribute effectively to sustainable development

Best practice — to demonstrate progress in environmental and resource management, and to share leading-edge practice

Global outreach — to contribute to a sustainable future for developing nations and nations in transition

Address   160 Route de Florissant
CH-1231 Conches-Geneva, Switzerland
Tel: +41 (22) 8393100   Fax: +41 (22) 8393131
E-mail: *info@wbcsd.ch*

**Foundation for Business
and Sustainable Development**

The WBCSD took the initiative to establish the Foundation for Business and Sustainable Development in late 1996 to encourage and fund major research and educational initiatives. *The Sustainable Business Challenge* is the first project initiated and co-funded by the Foundation.

Address   Foundation for Business and Sustainable Development
PO Box 301
Strandveien 37
N-1324 Lysaker, Norway
Tel: +47 67 589529   Fax: +47 67 581875
E-mail: *foundation@wbcsd.ch*

Acknowledgements

The Sustainable Business Challenge was launched by the Foundation for Business and Sustainable Development as a partnership effort between the United Nations Environment Programme, non-governmental organisations and industry experts. We all shared the wish to reach out to business students and young employees around the world to deliver the message that sustainable development matters for their work.

I should especially like to thank the following for their contributions to this process: Rick Bunch of the WRI; Prof. David Marks and his postgraduate Alliance Fellows; Alejandro Cano-Ruiz and Ilia Dubinsky from MIT; Jørgen Randers and his critically challenging colleagues at the WWF; Bertrand Charrier of Green Cross International; Prof. Phillippe Bourdeau of the Université Libre de Bruxelles; and Fritz Balkau of UNEP. In addition, Prof. Ulrich Steger from IMD and Prof. Bjarne Ytterhus from the Norwegian School of Management were willing to give an early draft the real test — trying the exam on their graduate students.

The initial funding of the project was provided by the Bellagio Forum for Sustainable Development, the Avina Foundation and the Rockefeller Foundation. In addition, several WBCSD members contributed financially to the initiative, including Novartis International AG, Ontario Hydro, 3M, BG plc, F. Hoffman LaRoche AG, Swiss Bank Corporation, General Motors Corporation, Noranda Inc., Storebrand ASA and Monsanto Company.

UNEP's Industry and Environment office in Paris, headed by Jacqueline Aloisi de Larderel, was a key partner in and sponsor of this project, contributing from its rich experience in environment and development. John Elkington of SustainAbility helped bring all the pieces — often highly controversial issues in themselves — together in a balanced way.

The editorial board included Kai Evensen, Peter Hindle and Silvia Pinal who contributed from their own long experience in the field, ably supported by Claudia Bergquist, Hans Christian Lillehagen, Charles Duff, and Peter Brigg of the WBCSD.

Last but not least, John Stuart and his team at Greenleaf Publishing have understood what we wanted and why it is so important to reach out to the next generation. They have been crucial in bringing our idea to fruition, combining the professionalism of a dynamic publisher with a broad understanding of environmental challenges. We could not have hoped for a more ideal co-partner.

Working at the business–environment interface, these individuals all see the problems business is facing and also the opportunities that business students have for making a difference.

And that's what *The Sustainable Business Challenge* is all about.

Jan-Olaf Willums
February 1998

Contents

Welcome to the Sustainable Business Challenge

DURING A RECENT BOARD MEETING, I found myself wondering what issues would be on the agenda twenty years from now. Two decades ago, in the late 1970s, environmental concerns were just beginning to enter the world's boardrooms. Today, environmental stewardship is part of the board member's vocabulary. How fully will environmental and social questions be integrated in the corporate fabric of an enterprise by 2020? That depends on those entering the corporate world today.

I am optimistic. I believe that, by the time today's business students have gained a senior position in the business world, concepts such as eco-efficiency and the 'social licence to oper-ate' will all be standard items on the board agenda.

How well prepared are you to meet the recruitment and career development requirements of 21st-century corporations? The WBCSD wanted to challenge business schools around the world to prove that their students have the quality of leadership and the business vision that the corporate world needs.

We therefore joined forces with AIESEC, the international student organisation, to launch *The Sustainable Business Challenge*.

First, we asked the corporate environmental staff of our member companies, as well as business professors and environmental activists, to help us bring together the facts and mate-rial they felt should be part of every student's understanding of the environment and devel-opment challenges.

Then we summarised these essentials in an Internet book — not a textbook but a guide to the minimum levels of knowledge business expects from students who are graduating from business schools and universities around the world and who want to succeed in the highly competitive worlds of industry, commerce and finance.

Finally, we formulated *The Sustainable Business Challenge Exam*, a multiple-choice test on the Internet. It is open to anyone wanting to demonstrate to future or current employers that he or she not only understands the issues and problems but also has a grasp of some of the emerging business solutions and opportunities. It is not an easy exam — it's a real challenge — and only about one-third pass it. The prize? A certificate signed by the WBCSD that con-firms that you have the knowledge and insight on how to run a sustainable enterprise.

The *Challenge* exam became an instant success. Within one month of the launch on UN's Earth Day in Korea in June 1997, several hundred had passed the exam. Now, more than a thousand visitors log on to the Website every day, and we have received enthusiastic e-mails from students, teachers and business people from places as far away as Croatia, Hong Kong and New Zealand.

Many urged us to supplement the Internet initiative with a book that would be equally useful for business practitioners looking for a primer on environmental issues. So we decided to adapt the Internet background document into a story of an imagined enterprise: the SDX Corporation.

This is the story of a corporation's search for sustainability, not an environmental man-agement textbook. Why? There are many good books and reports about the environment, and even more books about good environmental management. We are sure that you have read some of them. (However, to help you in your research, we have compiled a list of suggested further reading at the end of this book.)

This book is more like a sailor's weather map. It warns you where there might be rough sailing ahead and suggests where you can catch a good breeze. It reminds you in which direction the major trends — the trade winds — blow, what precautions you should take, and what equipment and provisions you should prepare.

It is also a road map to fact and information, warning you about roadblocks and suggesting interesting opportunities that you may meet on your way — like a travel book or Michelin guide for your future career.

But, most importantly, it contains the knowledge of business people involved in the WBCSD, who suggest how you can contribute to making business sustainable — that is, to helping it continue to be profitable and generate value in the long term.

We designed this book in partnership and dialogue with others. It will allow you to investigate the views of various stakeholders, from environmental groups to UN bodies, so you can devise your own path to meeting the sustainable business challenge.

So follow the story of SDX Corporation, meet the challenge and log on to the exam on *http://www.wbcsd.ch/foundation/*

Dr Jan-Olaf Willums became Secretary-General of the World Industry Conference on Environmental Management (WICEM II) in 1991, and of the ICC Industry Forum at the Earth Summit in Rio in 1992. In 1993, he became the head of the World Industry Council for Environment, which merged later with the Business Council for Sustainable Development to form the World Business Council for Sustainable Development where Dr Willums became Executive Director. Dr Willums is now with Storebrand, Norway's largest insurance company and one of Scandinavia's biggest investors and is President of the Foundation for Business and Sustainable Development. He is the co-author (along with Ulrich Goluke) of From Ideas to Action *(1992).*

Professor Jan-Olaf Willums
President
Foundation for Business and
Sustainable Development

Introduction

ARE YOU READY FOR A LITTLE TIME-TRAVEL? A visit to the corporate world of the 21st century? We would like you to join us to eavesdrop on an imagined dialogue within a virtual corporation questioning its future in a sustainable world. We have collected for you board papers, internal company memoranda and e-mails, letters and press clippings, all related to this virtual company which we have called 'SDX Corporation'.

We will follow the debate between Peter Kennedy, its Chief Executive Officer, and his Chairman Carlo Novoponte about strategy options, hear what Elizabeth Chang and the Corporate Planning people think about sustainable development, and understand why Heinrich Neubauer, the influential operations boss, wonders about resource efficiency.

Through these and many others' opinions and concerns, we want to highlight some of the key issues, facts and trends into the 21st century, which we believe any business student and employee of a corporation needs to understand.

If you join us, you may also see what possible board agendas you may have to cope with twenty years from now. They will be relevant both for a career in a multinational firm or in a small or medium-sized enterprise. They are no less relevant for those planning a career in government service.

Why do all those people — and in fact more and more key decision-makers in successful corporations around the world today — wonder and worry about sustainability? Because wherever you look, sustainability is now firmly on the international business agenda. *The Harvard Business Review* headlined the subject with two keynote papers in its first 1997 issue.[1] Three of the key messages were:

▶ 'If economic development means using more stuff, then those who argue that growth and environmental sustainability are incompatible are right. And if we grow by using more stuff, I'm afraid we'd better start looking for a new planet.'

▶ 'Far from being a soft issue grounded in emotion or ethics, sustainable development involves cold, rational business logic.'

▶ 'The achievement of sustainability will mean billions of dollars in products, services and technologies that barely exist today.'

Try to decide which of these statements came from an environmentalist, which from a business school professor, and which from the CEO of a major transnational corporation

The answer: none was from an environmentalist. The first two came from the CEO of Monsanto and the third from a professor at the University of Michigan. What this shows is that, as the business world wakes up to the nature and scale of the challenge, so business leaders are increasingly sounding like environmentalists. The key difference, perhaps, is that business has the resources to develop and deliver real-world solutions.

None of which is meant to suggest that this whole area will suddenly become controversy-free. Far from it. Controversies have played and will continue to play an important role in defining the emerging agenda for 21st-century business. That agenda will be strongly influenced by the *triple bottom-line*, by which is meant companies' performance in the environmental and social spheres as well as their traditional financial bottom-line results.

During our discovery trip, we will first explore how SDX Corporation — a rather successful medium-sized manufacturer of widgets (whatever they may be) based in the US — can remain successful in the 21st century. Peter Kennedy, the CEO, wonders how he can make his success last in the long term and apply sustainable development principles to his business strategy.

He quickly realises that SDX Corporation cannot find the best strategy unless he and his team clearly understand the key environmental issues and trends, and especially the topics that are on today's policy agenda. So he picks up briefings on the climate negotiations, water access politics and the biodiversity issue. As SDX is rapidly expanding abroad, he wants to know about global development challenges, as well as the emerging themes for international business.

If SDX is also going be a leader in its field twenty years from now, what are the new business concepts for the 21st century? And what management tools do the key staff of SDX — those young and bright people he is employing now — need to master?

At the end of our trip, we take a stop at a board meeting in the year 2020, and see what might be on the agenda at that time. How that future may look like depends very much upon you — our travel companions — and how capable you will be in meeting the challenges in your own career.

So please buckle up and focus your curiosity and imagination on how to make SDX a continuously successful corporation in the 21st century — and by that we mean a sustainable enterprise.

The SDX Executives "Cast List"

CARLO NOVOPONTE Chairman

PETER KENNEDY Chief Executive Officer

ELIZABETH CHANG Manager, Corporate Planning

INGRID PETTERSEN Vice-President, New Ventures

LI CHENG Vice-President, Corporate Finance

LAURA BENOTTI Manager, Government Relations

PIOTR KALINSKIJ Manager, Stakeholder Relations

HEINRICH NEUBAUER Vice-President, Operations

IRIS YABATA Strategy Unit, Chairman's Office

EDWARD LAWRENCE Director of Human Resources

JIM PETERS Director of Public Affairs

JOE MILLER Director of Communications

PROF. OKITO YAMAHASI Chief Scientist, SDX Technology Research Laboratory

CHUCK DOMANSKI Economic Unit, Corporate Planning

JOHANNES BAUER Corporate Legal Department

JACQUES PERRIER Management Education Advisor

SECTION ONE

The Sustainable Enterprise

> *The challenge for business is to keep up the momentum of continuous improvement in performance. This applies as much to the environment as to business results. But today environmental issues and the agenda for sustainable development have an increasingly international dimension.*
>
> Rodney Chase, Managing Director, British Petroleum

IN THIS FIRST section we want to find out how SDX understands patterns of change, and sees the emerging new business agenda. Why is leadership changing as we approach the end of this millennium? What are the drivers? And what is sustainable development all about? Ask Peter Kennedy, CEO of SDX, and you will know what business leaders look for when **recruiting tomorrow's leaders**.

The SDX board asked for some different perspectives on sustainable development, and will therefore be talking about:

> ▶ *The Tragedy of the Commons*
>
> ▶ *The Limits to Growth*
>
> ▶ *The Natural Step*
>
> ▶ *Industrial Ecology and Eco-efficiency*

Finally you will see how SDX can apply sustainable development to business strategy, and how scenarios can help our corporation in preparing for 'possible futures'.

Peter Kennedy
Chief Executive Officer

To: Board Members
Date: January 18, 2000

Subject: **How to remain successful in the 21st century**

The world is changing more rapidly and unpredictably than ever before. We face global economic, environmental and social challenges that will have a profound influence on the corporate sector in the new century.

- The companies that succeed in the future will be those capable of *learning and adapting quickly*, those that *can commit to big decisions with confidence* and can foster the *creativity and innovation* of their people. In other words, competence and knowledge will be the key competitive factors.
- Corporate social responsibility will be a focus of future corporate leaders who want to secure the "social license to operate."
- The policy framework will change. Business itself must play an active part in setting the framework, or others may set the agenda.

Clearly, all these trends will affect our strategy at SDX. So, in preparation for our next board meeting, I asked Corporate Planning to produce the attached background briefing. It should allow us to understand why some successful business leaders redraw the mental map of their corporations, and, more specifically

- What sustainable development means for business
- Why this must be important for the career of new employees

Given our full agenda, it's unlikely that we shall have time to cover all this at Thursday's meeting. However, we can at least begin the process and then return to discuss different aspects of it in more detail at subsequent board meetings.

Peter Kennedy

inter-office memorandum **sdx**

To:	Peter Kennedy, CEO <ptk>
From:	Elizabeth Chang, Manager, Corporate Planning <emc>
Date:	January 14, 2000
Subject:	**How to Remain Successful in the 21st Century**

First, some trends:

- Every year, almost 90 million people are added to the world's population — that's more people than live in Germany.
- By 2025, two out of three citizens will live in major cities, many of them in mega-cities with 10 million or more inhabitants. More than half will be teenagers.
- Natural limits for certain resources, for food production and for the planet's capacity to absorb waste seem to edge ever closer. Major technological breakthroughs are therefore needed to help tackle these problems.

Other trend-lines, no less dramatic, might equally well have been cited. The underlying message for the planet is clear: we can't go on indefinitely with business as usual. Things have to change.

The aim of this memorandum is alert the board to the strategic factors that may determine which companies will survive and prosper in the next century and which will go the way of sedan-chair manufacturers.

Understanding patterns of change

Successful leadership, be it in corporate management, finance or public administration, will require a different mix of skills than in the past. Managers in SDX will need to be able to recognize and understand trends and to navigate roadblocks effectively. They must be capable of developing efficient and/or innovative responses to key challenges. And they must be ready to profit from emerging opportunities.

A well-run company — or any organization for that matter — requires a vision of where to go. Our company therefore needs to agree on a common "mental map," on how it sees the future.[2]

What do we mean by a mental map?

- Mental maps are the lenses through which we look at the world.
- They reflect a set of assumptions about the way the world operates, what's important and what the future looks like.
- They are, for the most part, unchallenged. We probably aren't even aware that they are there.

But they make all the difference when making decisions.

A corporate mental map reflects the organization's collective view of the future. Are we in SDX sure that we all share the vision?

The phonograph is of no commercial value.

Thomas Edison, 1880

There is no reason for any individual to have a computer in their home.

Ken Olson, Digital Equipment Corporation, 1977

Even great minds can sometimes fail. Edison's assumptions about entertainment didn't allow him to see an opportunity for recorded music. Ken Olson, founder of DEC, defined too narrowly the nature of work, home and information.

Today, many people make decisions as if they believe that, with the advances of technology, there are no limits to natural resources nor to the capacity of our planet to absorb the waste we produce. They also act as if there is no interdependence between the global economy and the planet's ecological system.

These assumptions may have made sense when we were fewer people and our activities were on a small scale. But that is not where we are today.

This is where sustainability comes in. It fundamentally challenges our existing mental map and it helps us articulate a new one.

Elizabeth Chang

E.M. Chang

PS Enclosed 2 articles reviewing how business responded to these challenges.

VOL. VII   NO. 1   **JANUARY 2000**

FORWARD
INTERNATIONAL CORPORATE PLANNING

> Are we as a company ready for it? SDX's strategy has always been one of "staying ahead of the game." It's important that we don't fall behind in meeting the sustainable development challenge.
> P.K.

SUSTAINABILITY IN 2000

The Sustainable Management Challen

WHAT DOES sustainable development really mean? Is it anything more than a fashionable catchword? The first time the business world really woke up to sustainable development was in 1987, when many business leaders found a copy of *Our Common Future* in their in-tray.[3]

Produced by the World Commission on Environment and Development, chaired by Norwegian Prime Minister Gro Harlem Brundtland, the book reframed the environmental debate. Its key phrase was:

Humanity has the ability to make development sustainable – to ensure that it meets the needs of the present without compromising the ability of future generations to meet their own needs.

Our Common Future, 1987

Among the points made in the book were the following:

- Sustainable development is a *total concept*, providing an agenda, though not a blueprint, for action.
- It is a *process* of harmonizing resource use, investment,

> *Business must be profitable to survive, but it must also face the call to become sustainable to enable us all to survive.*
>
> Gro Harlem Brundtland

technological development and institutional change.

The shift to sustainable development must be powered by a continuing flow of *wealth* from industry. But future wealth creation will need to be much less environmentally damaging, more just and more secure.

The Brundtland Commission suggested *reviving growth*.[4] It said that sustainable development must tackle the issue of poverty because poverty increases pressure on the environment.

But the commission talked, too, about changing the *quality of growth*, that is to say making growth less materialistic, less energy-intensive and more equitable, so it could meet essential human needs for food, energy, basic housing, fresh water and health.

Crucially, the commission made it very clear that business has a

central part to play in all this. The phrase "paradigm shift" is probably over-used, but it is certainly appropriate here. For the first time, business was being seen as part of the solution, not simply as part of the problem.

The Brundtland Commission's report quickly raised interest among business leaders, because for the first time it suggested a partnership between government and industry.

Among business people, the concept of sustainable development itself was understood in many different ways. Some, for example, saw sustainability mainly as a technical issue, feeling reasonably comfortable with concepts such as eco-efficiency.

Others saw it as a social or political issue, arguing that issues around environmental justice or human rights need to be part of the equation.

Both of these perspectives are right. Over time, the agenda will inevitably change and, if history is any guide, expand. But the fundamental premise, the basis for the mental corporate map, is that we are part of a complex system which is not limitless but interconnected.[5]

How did business respond?

BY THE TIME the United Nations held its Earth Summit in Rio de Janeiro in 1992, business was already working towards understanding the nature and scale of the new agenda. Among the initiatives afoot were:

- The International Chamber of Commerce (ICC) launched the **Business Charter for Sustainable Development**, a set of 16 principles to guide company strategies and operations towards sustainable development. The ICC also created the World Industry Council for the Environment (WICE), a cross-sectoral group of 90 business leaders concerned with environmental challenges.

- Chief executives of 50 of the world's leading corporations formed, with Swiss industrialist Stephan Schmidheiny, the influential Business Council for Sustainable Development (BCSD) and launched its ground-breaking book *Changing Course*.[6] In 1995, the BCSD merged with WICE to become the World Business Council for Sustainable Development (WBCSD).

- In the UK, The Prince of Wales Business Leaders' Forum brought social responsibility into the debate on the environment.

- German industrialist Georg Winter created BAUM and the International Network for Environmental Management (INEM) to focus on hands-on environmental management solutions.

- A strong partnership developed between business and the UN Environment Program (UNEP), also involving business and industry in developing countries and transitional economies. It led later to the UNEP Banking Initiative and the UNEP Insurance Initiative.

What is clear today is that business took the initiative in the '90s and moved the agenda ahead, pushing for voluntary agreements and market instruments. The World Bank, UNEP and the OECD joined these initiatives on a partnership basis, as did some of the environmental organizations. Such alliances are likely to emerge as the more successful tools in the new century.

> *It has been argued that one cannot serve both the needs of industry and of the environment. I believe this is not an impossible task... However, a greener future will remain an idealistic dream unless industrialists and environmentalists meet to transform it into a reality by taking and sharing problems.*
>
> Martin Laing,
> Chairman, John Laing plc

The Green Business Network

A Monthly Briefing for Tomorrow's Business Leaders

Volume 3, Issue 1, January 2000

The Greening of Industry

What are the current trends?

OVER THE PAST TWO DECADES, major companies have been subjected to increasing pressure to improve their environmental performance. This arose from economic developments such as the energy crisis of the 1970s and from the growth in environmental legislation. The focus on hazardous wastes and emissions as well as accidental releases of chemicals mostly affected manufacturing operations.

Today, things are changing. Increasingly the focus is on *products*. There are nationally sponsored eco-label programs and restrictions on the use of hazardous substances such as chlorofluorocarbons, volatile organic compounds, or polyvinyl chloride (PVC).

Customers are demanding more environmentally-friendly products, which in turn is resulting in requirements for manufacturers to recover and recycle products at the end of the product's life.

Environmental credentials

Leading firms aim to achieve better market positioning, reduced costs and a greater degree of managerial control by being "ahead of the regulator."

Environmental credentials are an essential part of market positioning for many companies. Xerox, for example, believes that, in the long term, products can be marketed at least partly on the basis of environmental merit. Meanwhile, Hitachi's environmental objectives include increased customer satisfaction.

Manufacturers are responding to increased demand for products with less environmental impact as well as to stipulations by customers that they should take products back for recycling or disposal.

Retail establishments are placing similar demands on manufacturers.

Hitachi switched from glass-fiber-reinforced plastic to stainless steel in the manufacture of drums for washing machines in order to make the drums recyclable. The stainless steel drums are also stronger, allowing faster spinning, more effective de-watering of wet clothes and thus a lowering of energy consumption in the electric drier.

Unfocused pressure

While customers may be pressing for environmentally improved products, the pressure can be unfocused. Products marketed based on environmental performance have met with only limited success. To achieve success there have to be other benefits.

Ultimately, price and product performance are the key determinants of market share. Kodak, for example, increased the surface area of the silver halide particles in its film emulsion, thereby increasing the sensitivity to light and performance. Less silver halide is used per roll of film, but better photographs are produced. In addition, downstream film processors need smaller amounts of process chemicals, so reducing their costs and waste water discharge.

At Kodak, specific product design decisions are the responsibility of design engineers and business units. The front-line decision-makers have the resources to make informed decisions while maintaining their traditional autonomy. Using available implementation tools, they identify product-specific environmental concerns and balance them with product performance and cost specifications.

In this way, business units and design engineers apply their technical expertise and knowledge of product uses and markets to develop appropriate and cost-effective solutions tailored to the needs of their business and customers.

Xerox initiated a program of re-usable parts-shipping containers and pallets between its facilities and suppliers. This avoids 10,000 tons of waste and saves the company up to $15 million annually, in addition to saving timber resources.

Xerox also standardized its packaging for the shipments of parts between parts suppliers and facilities. More than 25 box configurations were replaced by nine standard boxes with common inserts that provide packaging flexibility. Sturdier construction allows these boxes to be re-used up to 15 times, and standardization results in less sorting for re-use. These packaging changes were achieved at a minimal cost to Xerox; they initiated the change and subsequently requested that suppliers implement the new standards.

Some companies have the added difficulty of not dealing directly with their ultimate customers. For example, intermediaries such as retail outlets may have difficulty accommodating design changes, even if final customers accept them.

At Kodak, retail outlets rejected a pilot project to eliminate packing boxes around film canisters that met with the approval of customers because the product was more difficult to stack and more easily stolen. Implementing such changes thus requires education and assistance within the supply-chain.

From the desk of
Edward Lawrence
Director of Human Resources

To: Katie Teasdale
Date: January 22nd, 2000
Subject: Recruiting Tomorrow's Leaders

Katie,

Sorry about this handwritten note, written en route to Dubai.

At the Board Meeting yesterday, we spent a fair bit of time discussing a paper written by Elizabeth Chang in Corporate Planning. Please get hold of a copy of the report from her and let me have your thoughts on its implications for our recruitment policy.

It's plain that the sustainability agenda is developing faster than almost any other part of the business agenda. Possession of the relevant understanding and skills will be a necessary condition for success in the 21st century. I believe SDX must take account of this in its recruitment and training policies.

Some of our potential recruits may take the view "Why should I care about sustainable development issues? My education has trained me to focus on economic and business challenges, not on saving the earth. And anyway, I don't want prospective employees to see me as an environmental activist."

This is misguided and out of date. At SDX, we expect new entrants to be attuned to the new business realities — and sustainable development is very much one of those.

Let's meet when I get back to hear your ideas.

Ted.

inter-office memorandum

sdx

To: Peter Kennedy, CEO <ptk>

From: Ingrid Pettersen, Vice-President, New Ventures <irp>

Date: January 27, 2000

Subject:

Defining sustainability

As the newest member of the Executive Committee, I took the liberty at last week's meeting to ask some "touchy" questions because I feel that SDX has always tended to focus too much on simply complying with regulations protecting the environment.

This is no longer enough: I believe we have to expand our vision to include sustainable development, a concept that goes far beyond end-of-pipe objectives. In short, we must become a "sustainable corporation."

In a company with our international spread, different people will naturally have different views of the world around them, including views about what is meant by being a sustainable corporation.

We therefore need to be clear about what a sustainable development strategy means for SDX.

To help clarify our ideas, I have prepared a short summary of some "mental models" of sustainability which we have used in the discussions with our "future technology" team.

I should be very glad of the chance to discuss the paper with you when you have a moment.

Ingrid Pettersen

Some Perspectives on
Sustainable Development

A report by Ingrid Pettersen,
Vice-President, New Ventures,
for
Peter Kennedy, CEO

January 2000

Some Perspectives on Sustainable Development

The "Tragedy of the Commons"

A short article in *Science* magazine in 1968 stirred up discussions and opened many people's eyes. Garrett Hardin, a professor at the University of California, argued in his article, "The Tragedy of the Commons," that a society permitting perfect freedom of action in activities that adversely influenced common properties was eventually doomed to failure.

Hardin cited as an example the tradition of a community pasture area, in New England called "the Commons," which could be used by any herdsman of the village. He pointed out that:

- Each herdsman, seeking to maximize his financial well-being, would wish to add an extra animal to graze the commons.

- In doing so, he would derive additional income from his larger herd and would be only weakly influenced by the marginal effects of overgrazing, at least in the short term.

- As every herdsmen would think alike, overgrazing would at some point destroy the pasture, and ruin all.

If we look around us today, we see many examples of the tragedy of the commons: the collapse of city transport in Bangkok and Tokyo, the overfishing of certain species of fish, or the overcrowding by tourists of resorts which were formerly places of natural beauty and serenity.

What we cannot see so easily for ourselves are the emerging strains on the *Global Commons*, such as the atmosphere.

When coupled with the first pictures of earth from space, which led to the view of the limited "Spaceship Earth," Hardin's article triggered an understanding of the close links between the environment and our economic activity. Those links are still as valid today. They underlie all three approaches we will review in this paper: "The Limits to Growth," "The Natural Step" and "Industrial Ecology."

1. The Limits to Growth

1.1 The concept

In 1972, the book *The Limits to Growth*, produced by an MIT team for the Club of Rome, focused the world's attention on the fact that many natural resources — among them fossil fuels, metals, timber and fish — are in limited supply and are in danger of being overstretched by current rates of consumption.

The study spoke both of physical limits and environmental limits. One example given was that the mining of ores, unless sensitively handled, could create increasing environmental disruption as more land is worked and more spoil requires disposal.

Although the computer modeling techniques on which *The Limits to Growth* was based were flawed and many of its direst forecasts have failed to be realized, the overall thrust of the book remains valid. Indeed, in 1991, a follow-up study by members of the same MIT team concluded that we are now, in the book's title, *Beyond the Limits*.

> *The ideas of limits, sustainability, sufficiency, equity, and efficiency are not barriers, not obstacles, not threats. They are guides to a new world. Sustainability, not better weapons or struggles for power or material accumulation, is the ultimate challenge to the energy and creativity of the human race...*

Meadows, Meadows and Randers, *Beyond the Limits*, 1991 [7]

1.2 The business reaction

The business world is not prepared to accept that there are limits to *economic* growth, but has come to realize that an increasing number of vulnerable resources, such as fisheries, *are* limited. In arriving at this position, business has very much taken account of the following factors:

- Market mechanisms, and especially innovation, have been strikingly effective in making available new sources of supply for those resources which, according to the forecasts, were expected to run out before the end of the 20th century.

- Markets have also been increasingly successful in reducing resource requirements and in controlling toxic and other unsustainable waste outputs from industrial processes.

- The real limit to economic growth within sustainable development is often in terms of human capital. This is not just the number of brains working on a problem, but also the availability of people who can think "out of the box" in order to come up with totally unexpected solutions.

The focus on nature's limits has, however, profoundly influenced many decision-makers, both in governments and in business, and has set the stage for "The Natural Step."

2. The Natural Step

2.1 The concept

First developed in Sweden by The Natural Step Foundation, this is a four-point philosophy that can be applied to any walk of human life — for example, to the management of communities, companies, industries, nations and ecosystems.

Its four basic principles, or "system conditions," are:

- Substances from the earth's crust must not be extracted at a rate faster than their slow re-deposit into the earth's crust.

- Substances must not be produced by society faster than they can be broken down in nature or deposited into the earth's crust.

- The physical basis for nature's productivity and diversity must not be allowed to deteriorate.

- There must be fair and efficient use of energy and other resources to meet human needs.

2.2 The business reaction

Many companies regard "The Natural Step" as a helpful distillation of a highly complex subject.

- The first three system conditions are based on natural science, but even so pose major challenges for such industries as mineral extraction and waste management.

- The fourth principle is slowly gaining wider acceptance in the business world, whereas a decade or so ago many might have felt the issue lay outside the realm of business.

> *Electrolux uses the total approach that considers the whole value-chain. The approach is aligned with our views of The Natural Step (TNS) as a practical tool. TNS gave us the legitimacy to take a step-by-step approach to the issue of refrigeration alternatives, instead of giving us reasons not to do anything in the short term.*

> Per Grunewald, Electrolux

3. Industrial Ecology and Eco-Efficiency

3.1 The concept

Industrial ecology and eco-efficiency argue for a "systems thinking" which places industry's focus on economic returns within an ecological and social framework.

Introduced by the WBCSD in the build-up to the 1992 Earth Summit, and subsequently refined, eco-efficiency involves the delivery of competitively priced goods and services which satisfy human needs and bring quality of life, while progressively reducing ecological impacts and resource intensity throughout the life-cycle, to a level at least in line with the earth's estimated carrying capacity. Or, more simply put, eco-efficiency is doing more, better, with less.

Central to this concept is the innovative drive, or what Claude Fussler of Dow Europe has called "Eco-Innovation."[8]

3.2 The business reaction

Many companies believe that industrial ecology and eco-efficiency make good business sense. This is because:

- They allow better corporate performance by taking account of the entire life-cycle of goods and services and increase the value for customers through the sustainable use of resources.

- No longer is it simply a question of pursuing recycling because recycling is "good," but of working to develop the best overall solution to a particular problem or challenge.

This approach also opens up a company's entire value-chain to scrutiny and improvement against eco-efficiency objectives. This is one of the most important keys to a sustainable economy, but we still need to work out how to use the market and its pressures to encourage evolution in the right directions.

Eco-efficiency contains both a vision and management tools for a green twenty-first century. If all business people and policy makers would follow, the world would be better off.

Ernst Ulrich von Weizsäcker, Wuppertal Institute

New emerging strategy and management concepts, among them the "triple bottom line," underscore the message that business must increasingly focus on integrating its targets and performance against the economic, social and environmental dimensions of sustainable development.

Ingrid

<<ends>>

Note: **Sections Five and Six outline how some of these challenges are being addressed by today's industry . . .**

inter-office memorandum

To: Peter Kennedy, CEO <ptk>

From: Iris Yabata, Strategy Unit, Chairman's Office <iy>

Date: February 3, 2000

Subject:

Applying sustainable development to business strategy

You asked for some thoughts on what we need to do, here at SDX Corporation to bring the sustainability concept down to real decisions and strategies that we can implement.

Sustainable development has three dimensions: economic, ecological and social.

The economic dimension
Sustainable development is about understanding the fundamental changes in the long term and looking at them as opportunities. As Professor Michael Porter puts it:

> *Environmental progress demands that we innovate to raise resource productivity — and that is precisely what the new challenges of global competition demand.*[9]

The ecological dimension
Sustainable development is about learning to value, maintain and develop our environmental *asset* so that we live off its *income*, not its *capital*. This means for us that we have to re-evaluate how our externalities will change, what it means for our sector, and how we should adapt to any possible new scenario.

The social dimension
Corporate social responsibility is about minimizing the company's adverse impact on the social and physical environment. It provides us with the *social license to operate*.

Let's evaluate these three dimensions in more detail:

We have to ask ourselves: Will people accept what we are doing in the long term? Have we listened effectively to all stakeholders?

P.K.

1. THE ECONOMIC DIMENSION

There are good business reasons why companies will gain competitive advantage in the long run if they adopt a strategy that embraces the three dimensions described above. Three of the key ones are discussed below. We also provide some examples of how this has been translated into action at some leading companies.

1.1. Raising competitiveness through innovation

Professor Michael Porter[10] sees the main effect on a company's competitiveness as being increased innovation:

- Today, globalization is making the notion of comparative advantage obsolete. Companies can source low-cost inputs anywhere and new, rapidly emerging technologies can offset disadvantages in the cost of inputs.

- Using resources productively is what makes for competitiveness today. Because technology is constantly changing, the new paradigm of global competitiveness requires the ability to innovate rapidly.

- This new paradigm has profound implications for the debate about environmental policy. It is important to use resources productively, whether these resources are natural and physical or human and capital

1.2. Gaining market share

In the future, more companies will strengthen their niches or sectoral positions by maximizing the environmental dimension. This again can have a direct effect on sales and market share.

> **When introducing a new line of trucks, VOLVO concentrated on publicizing the trucks' lower fuel consumption and lower emissions. Since then, Volvo's market share in that segment has grown by 35% in Europe, and operating margins in its truck operations are twice as great as its five-year average.**

But, as the following example shows, negative results are just as important as positive ones in getting a company to pay attention to the value-creating effect of environmental drivers.

> **In 1994, a rating of television sets by a Dutch consumer magazine included a review of four environmental dimensions — energy consumption, recycling, materials and use of harmful materials. The results placed NOKIA well above the traditional market leader, SONY. In one month, Sony's share of that market sector in the Netherlands fell by 12%, while Nokia's increased by 57%. Misjudging how consumers valued environmental considerations cost Sony nearly $1 million every quarter for one single product. The company has now taken the necessary steps to win back its market position.**

1.3. Adding to the bottom-line through resource efficiency

1.3.1. Reducing energy use

Improvements in energy and raw material productivity go straight to the bottom-line because they are direct cost factors.

> **NOVO NORDISK, a Danish biotechnology company, cut its energy consumption per unit of production by half over a period of five years. Its financial performance improved as direct result of that action.**

1.3.2. Reducing emissions, discharges and wastes on eco-systems

Manufacturing companies have seen a significant improvement in their financial performance (returns on assets, sales and equity) as a result of having reduced their emissions. But the financial improvement does not usually appear until one or two years after the reduction in emissions.

> **DUPONT'S Safety, Health and Environmental Excellence Award scheme is designed to encourage staff to bring to light opportunities for cutting emissions and waste. Over the past three years, these awards have generated more than U.S.$200 million in annual cost savings and revenue increases at DuPont and customer facilities, largely through reductions in emissions and wastes.**

1.3.3. Recycling or using "waste" material

It is possible to "close the loop" on the resource, even in traditional resource-based companies, while securing profits.

> **The founding idea behind DANISH STEEL WORKS was to transform scrap into steel. Over the years, the company has continued to develop its recovery know-how. As a result, it delivered an average operating profit of 8.7%, outperforming the market leaders and generating a better return than many companies on the *Fortune 500* list.**

2. THE ECOLOGICAL DIMENSION

The principles of sustainable development are being converted into ideas that business can understand and put to work. Do they add up to an identifiable change in course? We think that they do signal a paradigm shift in the way in which business does business. It is a shift from a fractured view of environment and development issues to a holistic view of business and sustainable development.

More specifically, this involves *shifts from*:

- Seeing only costs and difficulties in the concept of sustainable development to seeing savings and opportunities

- End-of-pipe approaches to pollution to the use of cleaner, more efficient technologies throughout entire production systems, and further, to seeing sustainable development as integral to business development

- Linear, "throughput" thinking and approaches to systems and recycling approaches

- Seeing environment and social issues as responsibilities only for technical departments or experts to seeing these issues as company-wide responsibilities

- A starting premise of confidentiality to one of openness and transparency

- Narrow lobbying to more open discussion with stakeholders.

These shifts are occurring at different speeds in different places, but they are all happening.[11]

3. THE SOCIAL DIMENSION

3.1. Issues and trends

The world's expanding population is one of the most problematic obstacles to the sustainable use of the planet's resources. World population is currently 5.8 billion and it is growing at a rate of one billion people every decade.[12]

Nearly all this growth is taking place in developing countries, making it increasingly difficult for them to provide adequate food, water, sanitation, education and employment.

Some more facts:

- In 1750, on the eve of the industrial revolution, world population had grown to about 800 million, an 80-fold increase in 10,000 years.

- The number of people living in poverty is also increasing. Currently, more than a billion people live in absolute poverty. The United Nations forecasts that this number will grow to 1.5 billion by 2025.

- About 1.8 billion lack basic health-care or access to safe drinking water, while more than 2 billion have no sanitation services.

- Many of the affected countries are seeing an explosive growth of mega-cities. This places intolerable strains on urban infrastructures, including the transportation systems, water, energy and food distribution systems, and on waste and sewage disposal systems.

*Development cannot be said to be sustainable if it is not equitable, or if it does not meet the **pressing needs** of the majority of the inhabitants of the globe.*

Brundtland Commission

Markets will play an important role in the sustainability transition. However, the world's poorest nations are generally unable to express their needs through markets.

This is why establishing good and effective government policies in developing markets is a critically important element if sustainable development initiatives are to reach the poorest.

- The world's richest 20% have over 60 times the income of the poorest 20% (compared with a multiple of "only" 30 in 1960).[13] Per capita income in Africa actual fell during the 1990s.

- All over the world, international TV is giving the poor a closer view of the world of the wealthy. If their hopes of higher living standards are thwarted, there could be massive social unrest.

Business has to tackle challenges such as these. The private sector is now almost universally recognized as the primary engine of economic growth and development. As a result, many governments of developing countries are encouraging liberalization, privatization and fiscal reform, and are emphasizing the importance of their countries participating more intensively in the world economic system.

This economic liberalization is helping to create much-needed wealth and more equality of opportunity. This in turn provides a foundation on which sustainable development can be built.

The World Bank predicts that, during the next decade, real economic growth rates in the northern economies will be 3% a year, while the developing economies as a whole will grow by twice that amount.

This depends on governments in the developing world exercising considerable economic discipline while continuing to liberalize their economies.

Huge amounts of capital will be needed to make such growth possible. A large portion will come from national savings but, according to consultants McKinsey, $2,000 billion will have to be imported.[14]

Iris Yabata

The attached news article pinpoints the rule of business in this area, which we at SDX must carefully evaluate.

at the end of this month.
The aim would be to help

last summer that one
should take over running

cannot be a ... it is not
only for the free movement

Can overseas investment bundled with aid help to transform the economies of developing countries?

Business and the multiplier effect of aid

**By our Business
Correspondent in Harare**

Funds from international development agencies – development banks and aid providers – represent a relatively small proportion of the total capital going into the developing economies, except into the very poorest.

But this aid can have an impact on policies and investment decisions in the developing world that is out of all proportion to the amount of funding. This is because an increasing amount of aid (from a steadily shrinking supply) is provided on the condition that policy reform takes place.

Aid flows are a sign of confidence in a country's prospects. Aid unlocks private capital, sometimes in a ratio of up to 6:1 for aid-supported projects. It can also be used to pioneer new approaches to financing which can be emulated by non-aid resources.

Furthermore, aid can mobilise financial markets to promote eco-efficiency in the developing world by means of a public–private financing partnership (to reduce risk for private investors), and also by financial-sector reform and privatisation.

Despite the fact that many developing countries still suffer extreme poverty and lack of investment, global investors are beginning to recognise the rapid growth rates and enormous changes in policy taking place in some of these areas.

In the 1990s, the developing economies have been enjoying pat-

terns of foreign direct investment (FDI) and portfolio investment that are more favourable than in the three decades since de-colonisation began.

FDI is fast replacing traditional development aid. As a proportion of capital flowing into developing countries, it has risen from 33% in 1991 to 75% in 1996. Emerging-market countries and companies are themselves directly accessing international financial markets and are raising substantial amounts of capital through bond issues in the Euro-markets.

The role of business

A key player in the drive to eradicate poverty and strengthen sustainable development in the developing world is the small or medium-sized enterprise (SME), so often the backbone of the local economy.

International business has a unique opportunity to work with the most progressive SMEs in these countries and to develop long-lasting partnerships with them.

One example of this is provided by The Prince of Wales Business

Leaders' Forum. A global network of business leaders, it has two main goals that are of direct relevance here.

The first is to raise awareness of the value of corporate responsibility to the successful management of international business and to the prosperity of host countries and communities.

The second is to encourage partnerships among business, government, communities, NGOs and aid agencies as an effective means of promoting sustainable development.

The Forum published a comprehensive report entitled *Business as Partners in Development*. Produced in collaboration with the World Bank and the United Nations Development Programme, the report describes hundreds of partnerships worldwide.

Another venture along similar lines is The Keidanren Nature Conservation Fund in Japan. It has promoted social partnership and helped local environmental NGOs to encourage social and regional development in developing countries in a sustainable manner. It has also helped to build a network which includes NGOs, the World Bank and the World Conservation Union.

The need for direct investment in developing countries goes to the very heart of the sustainable development challenge.

The developing world must have greater economic growth if it is to reduce poverty and disease, provide better education, develop industrial infrastructure, slow population growth and tackle local environmental problems.

This is what sustainable development is about.

Percy Barnevik,
Former CEO, ABB Asea Brown Boveri

inter-office memorandum

sdx

To: Peter Kennedy, CEO <ptk>

From: Elizabeth Chang, Manager, Corporate Planning <emc>

Date: February 7, 2000

Subject: ## Scenarios - Preparing for Possible Futures

You asked me to prepare a <u>forecast</u> of how environmental trends will affect our business. Unfortunately that is well-nigh impossible. What we can do, however, is to gain a better insight into the future by using scenarios.

For those who may not be fully familiar with this planning concept, scenarios are a tool that can help us to take a long view in a world of great uncertainty.

- Scenarios are designed to reflect the kinds of conditions in which we *may* have to do business.

- Scenarios are therefore not predictions, but descriptions of *possible futures*. They are used by many companies today to ensure that their strategies are robust and resilient across several possible future outcomes.

> *Scenarios are stories about the way the world might turn out tomorrow, stories that can help us recognize society and adapt to changing aspects of our present environment. Scenario planning is about making choices today with an understanding of how they might turn out.*[15]
>
> P. Schwartz

To understand better how the business world is changing, organizations such as the WBCSD and European Partners for the Environment (EPE) have developed scenarios that are intended not as predictions of a sustainable future but as tools for learning how to cope with possible futures.

We have recently formed a Scenario Task Force and we aim to come forward with some ideas specific to SDX within the next two months. In the meantime, by way of example, I am attaching an article highlighting the conclusions of a scenario exercise carried out recently by EPE and a paper from the WBCSD.

E.M. Chang

European Partners for the Environment

Three Scenarios for a Sustainable Business Future

The EPE scenario exercise suggests three distinct possible views about the future. Each in itself was regarded as consistent and possible; but not all of them were necessarily desirable.[16]

SCENARIO 1: NO LIMITS

Global environmental degradation has not materialised. Rapid technological innovation coupled with economic growth based on new clean industries, service and information technologies have generated the wealth to pay for a safe and clean development.

SCENARIO 2: ORDERLY TRANSITION

Environmental problems are serious. They are addressed with strong integrated economic and environmental policies. The role of regional governments (such as the EU) in setting targets, steering scientific programmes and ecological tax reform increases. Business is proactive and works closely in partnership with stakeholders.

SCENARIO 3: VALUE SHIFT

Scientific evidence and a series of environmental disasters lead to radical industrial and economic change. A bottom-up approach takes over where governments are ineffective. Social and ecological concerns are paramount and inspire a more caring, fair and vibrant community life.

All three scenarios envisage a challenge to business. Any one of them is plausible at this point in time. Although they are very different, some actions by

governments, business and other organisations would be of value in any scenario.

Most actions involve the capability to think long-term, integrate social needs, maintain a readiness to change and have the capacity to implement quickly and flexibly.

All the scenarios envisage increasing pressure to innovate and take social responsibility.

- In the *no limits* scenario, the driver will be competition from other companies as they introduce and build market leadership for their product and services.

- For the *orderly transition*, government will be an equal if not more important driver. As well as strengthening conventional regulation, it will create a regime where many environmental costs are internalised. Companies will get a mix of positive incentives and tough penalties to achieve environmental performance.

- The *value shift* scenario is inherently hostile to business. Only those that can, through innovation and social responsiveness, demonstrate their care for the new values will win and maintain a licence to operate.

Under all three scenarios the company that grasps the environment and development challenges early will be the winner. The tools? A greater competence on the part of the company, visionary leadership, and a willingness to secure the "social licence to operate" in addition to meeting the economic and ecological goals.

**World Business Council
for Sustainable Development**

The New, The Many,
The Connected

OF THE MANY possible scenarios that could be constructed in response to the challenge of sustainable development, all begin with three predetermined elements: the new, the many and the connected. These are the driving forces that shape the global business environment and will persist in any scenario. They form the common starting point from which the three stories emerge — and then diverge.

The New

Social and technological innovations lead to many new products and processes, and these will inevitably affect sustainability. Biotechnology, for example, offers an astonishing array of new opportunities and ethical choices. The Grameen Bank, which pioneered micro-credit agencies in Bangladesh, promises to have as great an impact on people's lives there as any development in technology. Even more, the synergy of these innovations interacting together will change our world in ways we can't predict. The information technology revolution, a driver of what is often called the "fifth wave" of technology, is only in its very beginnings.

In addition to social and technological innovations, another important area of the new concerns the economy, which has an increasing number of new players: new countries entering the global trading regime; new businesses; new partnerships among established businesses; non-governmental organizations (NGOs), which will assume a greater role in public debate and decision-making; the media, with its enormous power to sway public opinion, especially where emotions are high — and the unpredictable outcomes arising from many of these players interacting together in new ways.

Finally, we are at an essentially new moment in human history. For the first time, we are widely aware that our day-to-day decisions have the power to destroy our own habitat, the earth.

The Many

In the next 50 years, population will increase from 6 billion today to 9–11 billion. Material consumption will grow substantially, putting an enormous additional strain on already stressed ecosystems. This increase in people is accompanied by an increase in the diversity of the actors who influence how our societies and economies are shaped and what decisions we make.

The Connected

We are connected more closely and in more ways than we had previously realized, both to our fellow human beings and to the environment of which we are a part. As the power of our technology grows, as our communications infrastructure develops, and as our economic systems become more interdependent, we are creating a global "technosphere" to rival the global ecosystem. Its components are linked together in a myriad of different interconnections, so that what happens in any one area has the potential to affect many others. At the same time, this technosphere relies completely on the global ecosystem to provide the natural resources it uses and the sinks for the wastes that it produces.

The extent of our interconnectedness has changed the speed with which knowledge is transferred and problems are perceived — but not the speed with which these problems are solved. Social decisions are meditated by institutions that were designed for a slower, more methodical approach to solving problems, and these problems were assumed to come one by one. Now our problems seem baffling in their interlinked complexity, and the slow and insufficient response of our institutions leaves many people feeling frustrated and disillusioned.

Three Scenarios

Three scenarios have been developed to explore possible responses to the challenge of sustainable development. These responses arise from habitual patterns of thinking that form who we are, whether or not we are conscious of them. Such patterns or "myths" shape what we think is possible or real, and how we talk to one another about the crises and opportunities that face us.

Thus, the point of divergence from what all the stories have in common — the new, the many, the connected — arises when human actors respond in varying ways to the challenge of sustainable development. This variation in human response means that the branching point of the scenarios — what differentiates them from one another — lies not so much in the ecosystem or in the social system, but with us.

Will we simply ignore our social and environmental problems, trusting in the dynamic of economic growth and the innovations of technology, or, when problems reach a crisis point, will we turn away from our ineffective institutions of government and business to seek new models of governance that will take into account the religious and democratic values our narrow economic myth seems to ignore? Or will we try to embody our growing environmental and social values within the economic myth and experiment with ad hoc alliances and innovative forms in a world where everything we do is open for everyone to see and judge?

SECTION TWO

Key Environmental Issues and Trends

> *Even if all the companies in the developed world were to achieve zero emissions by the year 2000, the earth would still be stressed beyond what biologists refer to as its carrying capacity. Increasingly, the scourges of the late twentieth century — depleted farmland, fisheries, and forests; choking urban pollution; poverty; infectious disease; and migration — are spilling over geopolitical borders.*
>
> Stuart Hart, *Harvard Business Review*, 1997[17]

KNOWING THE FACTS is the basis for any good decision-making. In the environmental field, these facts seem often to be the object of heated debates. We have therefore invited scientists, environmentalists and industry researchers to summarise the core facts we feel everyone should be aware of.

In the following section you will therefore find a series of briefing notes that the determined chairman of SDX Corporation Carlo Novoponte expects any of his managers to know about. It is a condensed sweep through the most important environmental issues, covering

▶ *Atmosphere and climate.* What is the basis for today's political debate?

▶ *Water.* An area of increasing scarcity and conflict?

▶ *Fisheries.* Are we emptying this renewable resource?

▶ *Agriculture.* Can we feed the growing world population?

▶ *Forestry.* What are myths, what realities in the forest debate?

▶ *Biodiversity.* Are we losing the treasure of the future?

▶ *Energy.* How can we generate the fuel for economic development?

▶ *Transport.* Do we need mobility or access?

▶ *Waste.* A wasted resource?

After you have gone through these notes, you will easily understand why business leaders such as Carlo Novoponte want you to grasp both the challenges and opportunities for a business such as SDX — it's simply part of good management.

Carlo Novoponte
Chairman

To: Board Members
From: Carlo Novoponte
Date: February 18, 2000
Subject:

Strategy review: getting the facts right

Current patterns of development and resource utilization are not sustainable, as the Business Council for Sustainable Development noted in its book *Changing Course*.[18] In reviewing our long-term strategy, we must consider how the following concerns may affect our corporate future:

- ❏ Rapid population growth, especially in the developing world
- ❏ An accelerating and inefficient consumption of natural resources
- ❏ A related degradation of the productive parts of the environment, e.g. the depletion of fisheries and the loss of agricultural land, and a consequent loss of biodiversity
- ❏ Continuing pollution of the atmosphere, water and land, through the overuse or misuse of resources

In order to discuss these issues, we have to get the FACTS RIGHT. This is the purpose behind the attached briefings, which look at some of the most pressing environmental issues now facing us. Where the facts are unclear, we need to listen to the views of *various stakeholders* to understand the situation. And we must identify emerging trends early. I believe that looking at these issues from different angles will give us not only information but insight.

I look forward to a challenging debate at next Tuesday's board meeting.

C.J. Novoponte

... February 18th, 2000 ...

SDX Corporation, SDX Technology Park, Cambridge MA 10000
Tel: 617-000-1111   Fax: 617-000-1486   http://xyz.sdx.web

Strategy Unit, Chairman's Office

briefing note 00/02.01   February 2000

■ Atmosphere and climate

Life on earth is possible in large part because of the presence of the atmosphere. Apart from providing the oxygen upon which life depends, the atmosphere:

- Absorbs, distributes and re-emits solar energy. Some re-emission is held back by the atmosphere, which is part of the natural "greenhouse effect," keeping average temperatures at levels suitable for life as we know it.

- Shields all forms of life from harmful ultraviolet (UV) radiation, thanks to its protective stratospheric ozone layer.

This thin layer of gases is today being affected by human activities as never before. Despite decades of warnings about air pollution and of legislated efforts to control it, we see that:

- Combustion of fuels and other materials is still causing extensive local and transboundary air pollution.

- Urban dwellers are still being exposed to potentially injurious levels of toxic substances.

- Some forests are still being degraded by acid depositions.

- Emissions of halocarbons are thinning the ozone layer.

- Greenhouse gases (mainly carbon dioxide [CO_2] emissions from transport and power generation but also methane from waste dumps, cattle and rice fields) are still accumulating in the atmosphere – with the risk of drastic long-term climate changes.

■ Policy responses

Local air quality will remain an urgent priority in the developed world and is also in the process of becoming an urgent priority in many transition economies and developing countries, where the damage caused by air pollution is believed to be as much as 2–3% of GNP.

In 1987, governments signed the **Montreal Protocol** to the Vienna Convention for Protection of the Ozone Layer. This defined specific target reductions and a clear timetable that now calls for all production and consumption of Ozone-Depleting Substances (ODSs) to cease in the industrialized world by 2000.

The **UN Framework Convention on Climate Change**, signed by 120 countries in 1992, sets out the major directions and objectives for reducing climate gas concentration in the atmosphere. It is built on a *"precautionary approach"* – i.e. policy action taken *before* the underlying science has reached absolute clarity.

The **Intergovernmental Panel on Climate Change (IPCC)** was established by the World Meteorological Organization (WMO) and the UN Environment Program (UNEP) in 1988 to assess the available scientific, technical and socio-economic information in the field of climate change. In 1995, the group's Second Assessment report to the UN Framework Convention concluded that climate change could be rapid, have adverse impacts and was caused by "discernible human influence."

Based on these scientific conclusions, governments are negotiating policy measures in industrialized countries to *reduce* greenhouse gas emissions by 2010. This is a commitment that goes beyond the stabilization objectives for 2000, which only few nations will achieve.

■ Business challenges and opportunities

In the case of local and regional air quality, industry has made considerable progress in dealing with stationary pollution sources. Progress has also been made with mobile sources but, despite a growing consensus on the health and ecological impact of vehicular emissions, the underlying trends remain worrying in many parts of the world.

Given sufficient certainty, industry can move to tackle even the most extraordinary challenges. Less than a decade ago, CFCs were entrenched in the industries of the U.S., yet "with considerable ingenuity and aggressive investment in innovation, many U.S. industries eliminated CFC use more quickly, at lower cost, or with greater environmental benefits than observers once predicted."[19]

Among the challenges still facing us, however, is the continuing use of ozone-depleting substances in countries outside the Montreal Protocol and in the booming black market. The biggest supplier of black-market CFCs is Russia, although India and China are also still major producers. Clearly, policing of international environmental rules remains a critical issue.

The greenhouse gas threat is still the major challenge for business on a global scale. Some actions to slow climate change will be virtually cost-free, but most will involve spending scarce funds with inevitable opportunity costs. Faced with fast-growing populations, most developing countries have not yet been willing to commit to the necessary changes.

Note: **This issue is explored more fully in the section on Climate Politics in Section Three . . .**

Strategy Unit, Chairman's Office

briefing note 00/02.02   February 2000

■ Water

■ The freshwater problem

Although three-quarters of the earth is covered by oceans, only a small fraction is readily available for human consumption: 97% is saltwater in the oceans, and the vast majority of the remainder is locked up in ice caps and glaciers or as groundwater. Unchecked withdrawal of freshwater reduces the amount available for use as drinking water and leads in coastal regions to increasing salinization of the remainder. Human activity is also a major cause of damaging flood hazards.

☐ Freshwater supply

The following facts are relevant:

- About 70% of all freshwater is used for agricultural purposes, specifically irrigation. Industry withdraws around 25%, and domestic and municipal use accounts for the rest.

- Half of all agricultural water is lost to the sea without being captured for recycling.

- One-third of the population of the developing world lacks safe water for drinking and sanitation. Because 80% of all diseases are water-borne, lack of clean water constitutes a global public health crisis.

- Many developing countries, with annual per capita consumption as low as 50m^3 (compared to 2100m^3 in the U.S.), will have to increase freshwater use in the future.

Pressure on local water sources is increasing as cities grow. Even relatively developed mega-cities, such as Mexico City, face massive challenges. With 20 million inhabitants, Mexico City largely depends for its water on an underground aquifer, which is rapidly being depleted. Other linked problems are the loss of up to a third of the city's supply through cracked pipes and extensive water contamination – more than 90% of liquid industrial waste is still discharged untreated into the sewer.

However, the crisis now becoming apparent in many parts of the world is not due to a decline in the resource as such, but due to lack of capital and infrastructure investments. **Water quality** will therefore be a growing global concern and industry has to expect increasingly tougher regulations:

- Regulatory and monitoring programs, regional programs and legally binding agreements have been launched. Two examples are the London Dumping Convention and the Mediterranean Action Program.

- We can expect more stringent liability and compensation regimes covering pollution damage from shipping and dumping activities, including regimes for hazardous substances carried by ships.

■ Marine pollution

Between three and four million tons of oil enters the oceans annually. Shipping accidents, although very visible and widely publicized, account for only one-eighth of the total. Oil released by accident, or as part of deliberate routines in "normal" marine transportation activities, is estimated to be about three times the amount spilled by ship disasters.

The result is that input of nitrogen compounds, particularly from fertilizers, sewage and combustion processes, result in the loss of valuable fisheries. This is happening with disturbing and increasing regularity in "enclosed" marine environments such as the North Sea and the Mediterranean. Regulatory and monitoring programs, regional programs and legally binding agreements have been launched, such as the London Dumping Convention and the Mediterranean Action Program.

We can expect more stringent liability and compensation regimes covering pollution damage from shipping and dumping activities, including regimes for hazardous substances carried by ships. Oceans are currently the focus of an Independent World Commission which has as its aim the implementation of an Ocean Convention and will undoubtedly raise awareness of issues associated with the use of freshwater resources.

■ The politics of water access

Access to water will increasingly become a politically sensitive issue that will directly affect business decisions of plant location, but will also influence the general investment climate. Today, 40% of the world's population lives in the more than 200 river basins shared by more than two countries.[20] As the demand for scarce water resources grows as a result of increasing population, the potential for escalation in regional conflict is apparent. Examples of such conflicts have already occurred over shared water resources of the Jordan, Tigris, Euphrates and Nile rivers in the Middle East, and the Indus and Ganges rivers in Asia.

■ Policy responses

A UN Water Convention is not at this time generally considered to be feasible because of significant tensions over water ownership in many parts of the world. However, the UN will develop principles to guide global water resource management – a precursor to the development of a Convention in the future.

In developing countries, establishing a water policy to protect the environment – in particular water quality for new development projects – is a rapidly growing priority.

■ Business challenges and opportunities

The industrial and commercial demand for water is increasing rapidly; demand is forecast to double by 2025.

The trend toward closed manufacturing processes and regulations will progressively reduce poorly treated industrial discharges.

- Current market prices for water do not reflect its true economic and environmental value. Economic instruments (for example, tradable permits) would ensure that users pay the full cost of using and treating water.

- Since most water used by industry is for cooling and cleaning purposes rather than for actual consumption, water savings can still be realized. Equally important are the potential savings in agriculture.

A recent study by the World Business Council for Sustainable Development suggests that industry has a much larger role to play than just protecting its ability to use water. Industry brings the technological capability to move and treat water and manage water supplies.

■ Fisheries

In addition to our air and water resources, a wide range of renewable and non-renewable natural resources are now under severe pressure. One example is the world's fisheries:

- Worldwide, fish and other marine products account for 16% of the animal protein consumed, more than either pork or beef.

- But the total global catch has fallen in all but two of the world's 15 major marine fishing regions – and in four of them by more than 30%.[21]

- It is estimated that the world's fishing fleet is double the size it needs to be to make the annual catch, partly due to large national fleet subsidies. It is far from certain that this catch is itself sustainable, long term.

■ Policy responses

As one of the great global commons, the oceans should fall within the realm of international governance, but a key problem here has been working out who has jurisdiction over particular areas of water.

The biggest responsibility for managing fishing activities falls to the coastal nations themselves. They control the resources within 200 miles of their shores – the so-called Exclusive Economic Zones. Ocean resources beyond this limit remain a common property resource.

Unfortunately, fish don't respect the arbitrary boundaries that nations establish and many fish stocks migrate between jurisdictions.

- The first real steps towards curtailing the ability of fishing vessels to fish anywhere they liked was the Third United Nations Conference on the Law of the Sea, at which governments agreed to establish a zone, no more than 200 nautical miles wide, within which coastal nations would have sole rights to natural resources.

- The Food and Agricultural Organization (FAO) developed in 1995 the Code of Conduct for Responsible Fisheries, a voluntary set of principles and practices to help coastal nations establish sustainable fishing policies.

In spite of these efforts, global fishing practices are still highly environmentally destructive and wasteful. Roughly 25% of the total fish harvest is simply discarded as being too small, the wrong species, etc.

At the **national level**, many government subsidies have been counter-productive in terms of achieving globally sustainable management of fishery resources.

Leading research institutes hold that government policies over the last 40 years have led to a pattern of exploiting global fisheries, based on *mining the resource*, which is unsustainable.

■ Business challenges and opportunities

The fishing industry in the developed world can scale down its fishing fleets in line with scientifically suggested limits, leading to limits on vessel numbers and catch sizes, or it can start the long haul towards the sustainable exploitation of the world's fisheries.

One answer is to ensure the better management of existing marine fisheries, for example by using *market forces* to encourage the transition towards more sustainable fisheries. Individual Transferable Quotas (ITQs) are one such market-based approach that seeks to give those in the fishing industry some financial stake in preserving and rebuilding fish stock.

Unilever, the company behind such brands as Bird's Eye and John West, is trying another approach. As the world's largest fish buyer, it is backing a plan, developed jointly with the WWF, to set up an international labeling scheme that identifies sustainable fish production. All the company's fish products will be labeled by 2005.

The new standards, which will be policed by a new **Marine Stewardship Council (MSC)**, will focus on two main issues: where the fish are caught, and the methods used to catch them. Participating fisheries will be certified against the MSC criteria and their packs will bear the MSC logo.

Aquaculture, or fish farming, has often been put forward as the answer to these problems. Certainly, it is emerging as a significant economic force and, potentially, as one answer to the problems of the world's "wild" fisheries. Over time, it may well become a major source of fish and other marine products.

However, raising salmon in a fjord in Norway is different from raising shrimps on the coast of Ecuador, and each has a different effect on wild fisheries. The challenge is to avoid poorly managed aquaculture that causes problems such as the destruction of coastal habitat, nutrient and pesticide pollution, and genetic contamination of wild fish populations.

briefing note 00/02.04   February 2000

■ Agriculture

The issues affecting the agricultural sector range from questions about how more food can be produced to the longer-term sustainability of the systems and processes used to produce it. Some facts:

- More than 800 million people are undernourished today. About 180 million children suffer from malnutrition.

- Even though 1.5 billion more people are adequately fed compared to thirty years ago,[22] population growth continues to make the food issue a rising challenge for society.

The growth in food supply has more than kept pace with population growth since 1950. In fact, in developed countries overproduction has dominated in recent years. On average, food as calories per capita has increased continuously in developing countries. However, shortages of food are common in sub-Saharan Africa – where supply has declined in recent years – and in South Asia. This is mainly due to poor infrastructure, political unrest and low investments in agriculture and agricultural research.

Part of the problem is also due to considerable losses during harvesting, storage and transport of food products. Yields are low and often declining because more and more marginal and poor land with either low productivity or prone to erosion has had to be used for crop production.

Often, the soil is mined for nutrients, causing yields to continually decline. One cause is that plant residues and manure are burnt instead of being incorporated into the soil in order to maintain soil organic matter.

■ Policy responses

In developed countries the main emphasis has been on reducing the adverse effects of intensive agriculture on the environment. For example:

- Restrictions on the use of manure and sewage sludge

- Precision farming and integrated fertilizer and pest management

- Set-aside of agricultural land prone to erosion or other degrading effects

Organic production has been emphasized as an environmentally-friendly mode of food production due to lower inputs. Seen from a developing-country perspective, however, lower inputs lead to lower outputs which does little to address the need for increased food global security. At the same time, an agriculture that mines the soil for nutrients and is expanding into more and more fragile areas is hardly sustainable.

Besides waste due to poor management in developing countries, overproduction has dominated in developed countries in later years, complicated by controversial programmes such as the European Common Agricultural Policy.

■ Business challenges and opportunities

One of the challenges in agriculture is to improve world food supply simultaneously with improvements in its sustainability. Business contributions will focus on:

- **Best agricultural practices**, which include combining careful husbandry with farming inputs in ways that care for environmental interests while producing sound economic farming operations. This is to a large extent a question of education and information. Major partnership programs between governments and industrial producers are addressing this issue worldwide. The business opportunities lie in finding the right agricultural practices for the local conditions.

- **Integrated pest management (IPM)** techniques, which carefully manage the use of pesticides together with biological measures in order to reduce damage by pests and keep disease to a minimum. The biological methods include crop rotation and multicropping, biological control using natural predators and "trap crops" (which lure pests away), timing of planting, and appropriate use of water and fertilizers.

- **Infrastructure improvement** in developing countries where soil degradation and the negative nutrient balance is caused by the lack of availability of farming inputs, such as fertilizers and financial credit.

- **Biotechnology**, whether used in developing new or improved crop plants or animal strains, is more controversial. Some argue that genetic engineering and modern forms of biotechnology have no place in sustainable agriculture. Others contend that sustainable agriculture will only be possible if we use such techniques.[23] Instead of using major quantities of destructive pesticides, for example, the crop can be designed to defend itself by inserting the gene for a microbial protein that is only toxic to specific pests. Monsanto has developed new forms of potato and cotton, bioengineered to protect themselves against the Colorado beetle and the cotton budworm respectively.

The key challenge for the agricultural industry, and its regulators, will be to ensure that the use of modern agricultural techniques contribute to agricultural and environmental sustainability – and that any risks to human health and safety, and to the environment, are kept to a minimum.

briefing note 00/02.05   February 2000

■ Forestry

Forests cover one-third of the earth's land surface. Three-quarters of those forests are outside OECD countries. The following facts are relevant:

- Trees have a profound effect on *local climates* by absorbing and releasing water vapor, while their root structures provide *soil stability*, which helps to prevent erosion.

- Forests also provide immense *economic benefits*. The annual value of world timber production for all uses – as timber, paper and fuelwood – amounts to over $300 billion. Forests, too, are the source of a wide range of medicinal compounds.

- The paper industry is the third largest industry in the world. Alone, it contributes 2% of world trade, totalling about $260 billion in sales, and it employs 3.5 million people.

Although the "information revolution" is here, it has not yet led to a decrease in paper use. There is a clear need for paper in our lives – for education, communication, printing, hygiene, packaging and even for the growing needs of the "paperless" computer society.

■ Deforestation

While the wooded areas in most OECD countries have stabilized in the last 20 years, the rate of deforestation in developing countries has accelerated. The world's forest areas could possibly be reduced by as much as one-third within the next 40 years if appropriate action is not taken.

The **tropical rain forests**, which span the equator in Africa, the Americas and Asia, cover only 6% of the earth, yet they are host to half of all living species. These forests have been under increasing pressure both from logging and, increasingly, from clearance and other activities arising from local population growth and agriculture.

Rather than disputing the rates of forest loss, the challenge today is to work out ways of slowing and then reversing these trends.

■ Policy responses

There have been numerous efforts to tackle forest loss. Some have worked, but most have done little to change the overall trend:

- The Tropical Forestry Action Plan, the International Tropical Timber Agreement and the International Tropical Timber Organization have so far failed to halt the destruction, as has the Intergovernmental Panel on Forests.

- At the Rio Earth Summit in 1992, efforts to launch a Framework Convention on Forests failed. A compromise UN Statement of Forest Principles has not had any major impact.

Effort is still needed in national forestry plans, in land-use planning, in developing sustainable forestry principles, criteria and indicators, and in public education.

■ Business challenges and opportunities

Key factors in driving the transition towards sustainable forest management include forest and product certification schemes, industry association codes of practice, environmental quality management systems and internal audits.

- Certification schemes such as the Forestry Stewardship Council (FSC), developed by WWF and its partners (among them forest management companies, timber users and retailers), have an important part to play.

Many of the negative views about the paper and forestry industries are based on out-of-date or incomplete information, and have in some cases caused industry to adopt practices that waste money for negligible environmental gains.

To get at the facts, the WBCSD commissioned the International Institute for Environment and Development (IIED), an independent research body, to carry out the most comprehensive study to date of the entire paper cycle, from forestry and paper manufacture through to paper's end-use, recycling and ultimate disposal. The report, **Towards a Sustainable Paper Cycle**, answers key questions of relevance to business, government and society. Among the report's findings were:

- Although paper consumption will double over 50 years, there is enough wood fiber to meet this expected growth, assuming development of new wood plantations in the tropics and sub-tropics continues.

- Perhaps the most interesting and controversial finding was that *recycling is not always the panacea* many believe it to be. Although recycling waste paper has environmental benefits compared with dumping it in landfills, a greater environmental return can sometimes be achieved by incinerating the paper and harnessing the energy it releases.

More and more forest companies are experimenting with shifting their businesses to a more sustainable pattern.

Strategy Unit, Chairman's Office

briefing note 00/02.06   February 2000

■ Biodiversity

The world's biological resources are used everyday by industry – for example, in agriculture, pharmaceuticals and forestry.

Wild plants and animals are vital to human survival. Science is constantly discovering new ways in which biodiversity can help alleviate human suffering.

Conserving the genetic species and ecosystem assets of the world will help to improve and sustain the quality of life. But the activities of a rapidly growing human population are destroying natural habitats at an accelerating pace.

Biodiversity *is defined as the variability among living organisms and the ecological complexes of which they are part, including diversity within and between species and ecosystems.*

UN Convention on Biological Diversity

Although only 1.4 million species of life on earth have been described, it is estimated that there are at least five to ten million, and perhaps as many as 100 million species on the planet. Many of them are found in tropical forests.

Although the development of new species, and the extinction of old, has been a continuing process since life first emerged on the planet, there are some worrying trends today:

- The rate of extinction has increased. Species that have evolved over millions of years are disappearing at rates estimated as high as 100,000 a year.

- If current rates of extinction continue, some scientists forecast a 15–30% loss of wildlife worldwide over a ten-year period.[24]

- Because 50–90% of all species live in the tropical forests, the continuing deforestation in the tropics poses the main threat to biodiversity.

■ Biosafety

The **transfer** and **manipulation** of genetic materials from plants and animals, through biochemical means, has brought many advances to medicine, agriculture and industry. At the same time, people are concerned about the potential risks to biodiversity and human health posed by living modified organisms (LMOs) – the term used in the Convention to define organisms that have been modified through biotechnology.

■ Policy responses

Some 40 countries have developed national biodiversity strategies. The objectives of the **Convention on Biological Diversity**, signed in Rio in 1992, are:

- The *conservation* of biological diversity
- The *sustainable use* of its components
- The *equitable sharing* of its benefits

These broad objectives will likely affect all business sectors by:

- Restricting long-term access to land and biological resources
- Imposing more stringent environmental impact assessments
- Introducing restrictions on the trade in biological products

Some countries already possess legislation designed to ensure the safe use of living modified organisms (LMOs). The greatest concern revolves around the absence of rigid field-testing of LMOs, as the interaction of these organisms with other natural species is unknown. Work is under way to develop biosafety guidelines to ensure that correct field-testing and handling of LMOs takes place.

■ Business challenges and opportunities

At least 35,000 species of plants are estimated to be of medical value, yet just 5,000 have been studied in detail for medical applications. Surveys in the United States show that 11% of the top 150 prescription drugs were originally derived from living organisms. Nine of the top ten prescription drugs are based on natural plant products.

The World Health Organization estimates that 80% of the people in developing countries rely on traditional plant-derived medicines.[25] China produces more than 40,000 different traditional plant drugs.

The pharmaceutical industry has started using the royalty concept. One of the first examples was in Costa Rica. Merck & Co., a U.S. pharmaceutical firm, signed a contract to pay the National Biodiversity Institute of Costa Rica a 2% royalty on sales of any new medicine developed from the institute's samples. The agreement involves Costa Rica granting a limited, non-exclusive license to Merck which allows it to explore Costa Rican biodiversity for new medicines. In addition, Merck has agreed to pay $1 million dollars up-front.

This new type of partnership agreement provides financing that developing countries need to preserve that biodiversity. Glaxo-Wellcome, Novartis and others have developed similar partnership arrangements.

■ Energy

Energy supply and demand have been at the center of many of the major environmental and sustainability controversies of the past couple of decades. For example:

- During the 1970s, with the publication of the Club of Rome's *The Limits to Growth* study and successive OPEC oil shocks, energy supply occupied center-stage politically. At the time, the key question was how quickly supplies of fossil fuels would run out.

- New industries have grown up around energy efficiency and renewable energy supply, although relatively low energy prices have slowed momentum in both areas in recent years.

- By the late 1990s, attention had switched to another set of constraints: global warming and other forms of environmental change.

■ Policy responses

Today, oil prices are lower than they were in 1973. There is abundant supply, partly because of the rapid development of new exploration technology, making new offshore resources accessible in Alaska and the North Sea, and extracting even more oil from existing fields. The abundance of coal in rapidly developing countries such as China and India, and utility regulation in the North[26] suggest that fossil fuel's share is unlikely to fall below 80% before 2017. Inevitably, further new fields will be found, although their development will sometimes be controversial – as would be the case with the U.S. Alaskan National Wildlife Refuge (ANWR) area or the "Atlantic Frontier."

Economists argue that a carbon tax would be the easiest way to reduce the demand for energy. The infrastructure in the industrialized world has, however, been built on the easy access to oil, making the demand elasticity less suitable for changing easily to other forms of energy. The competitiveness of many countries has also been built on access to cheap energy, making governments reluctant to change the energy infrastructure unilaterally. A properly planned slow ecological tax reform (i.e. moving taxes from labor to scarce or polluting resources) would, however, move the energy mix towards more sustainable sources.

Some major oil companies are already investing heavily in alternative energy technology: BP Solar is already the world's largest producer of photovoltaic cells. Shell, Amoco and Enron are other key players that believe in long-term opportunities as broad-based energy companies. Both the U.S. and European Governments are increasing their support for non-fossil-fuel technology, and are beginning to design more policies encouraging alternative fuels, such as the Non-Fossil-Fuel Obligation in the UK, or the Zero-Emission requirements scheduled for a certain percentage of cars sold in California.

■ Business challenges and opportunities

Energy efficiency is a key part of eco-efficiency. This suggests that the future will see a return of attention to the energy agenda. For this to happen, however, fossil fuel prices will need to rise.

Demand-Side Management (DSM) is one area of activity that could well become much more important in the coming decades. The energy industry, particularly the power utilities, can help reduce demand by promoting better energy management so that the need for new peak capacity investments is decreased. Handled properly, this *negawatt* objective, as Amory Lovins called it,[27] can result in new revenue.

In the developed world, the two main uses of energy are transportation and the provision of heat and power to domestic buildings. Both of these consume substantially more energy than is used by industry, a reversal of the situation only 15 years ago. This partly reflects greater energy efficiency in industry, but it is mainly attributable to increased energy use in the other sectors.

Cars are major consumers of energy, but are becoming progressively more fuel-efficient:

- A new car will today travel, on average, one-third further on a gallon of fuel than a car with the same engine size made in 1975. Over the next decade, a further 10% improvement in fuel economy is expected.

- But the number of cars in use continues to rise inexorably, which suggests that other strategies will also be necessary. For example, the Rockefeller Foundation is promoting the development of a large market for electric cars and buses for areas where electricity can be produced from renewable sources.

Co-generation, which involves the simultaneous generation of heat and power, is another bright hope. Potentially, it offers a conversion efficiency of up to 90%,[28] considerably more than twice that of present coal-fired power stations.

Although co-generation produces the lowest-cost energy among the fossil-fuel-generating options, and the lowest carbon emissions, it generates only around 7% of the EU's total electricity demand. But, underscoring co-generation's potential, this figure rises to more than 30% in environmentally proactive countries such as the Netherlands, Denmark and Finland.

■ Transport

Transport is a prerequisite for social and economic development and is thus an integral part of it. As a result, the need for transport rises with economic growth, and the availability of transport helps generate economic prosperity.

Although the economic and social benefits of transport are undisputed, its environmental effects are becoming increasingly of concern. The growth in the demand for transport has become a major issue in all developed, and in many developing countries. This trend has become one of the most significant threats to the environment.

As an indication of the scale of change, in 1950 there was one car for every 46 people worldwide. Despite a doubling of world population over 40 years, by 1990 ownership had reached one for every 12 people.[29]

The effects come in many forms. There are, for example, the land-use implications of setting up the transport infrastructure, including the roads, rail tracks and airport runways.

Major strides have already been made in cleaning up vehicle exhausts, thanks to a combination of better engine technologies and emission control systems. But successes here can lead to second-order problems, such as when the shift from leaded to unleaded petrol removed a large part of the lead burden but increased exposure to benzene, a chemical present in higher concentrations in unleaded fuels.

As vehicle emissions build up in cities, they react with sunlight to cause problems linked to low-level ozone (photochemical smog) which, a growing body of evidence suggests, has severe health implications.

Given that there is a clear and continuing link between increasing wealth and the desire for mobility, there is unlikely to be any end to this trend in the foreseeable future. Indeed, some forecasts suggest that the current world car fleet of 600 million will reach around one billion by 2015.

■ Policy responses

Given that different transport modes produce very different effects per passenger-kilometer or ton-kilometer traveled, governments have tried to tilt the balance in favor of particular modes – notably rail transport.

However, none of this has been enough to mitigate the overall environmental effect, especially in the rapidly expanding cities in developing countries.

The future may see a range of policy measures, including integrated transport policies, road and fuel pricing, targeted subsidies of public transport, and international liaison on long-haul routes. Limiting car use in inner cities, such as in Oslo, are policy measures already successfully up and running aimed at changing patterns of car use.

The future will also include strong R&D efforts focused on identifying next-generation technologies, and increasingly stringent emission standards on both cars and aircraft.

■ Business challenges and opportunities

Most car companies are concentrating more on the "greening" of their products. Some are thinking in broader terms:

- Volvo focuses on transport efficiency, including better co-ordination of goods distribution, intelligent transport systems, and bus lanes.[30]

- Many companies, including Fiat and Honda, offer electric vehicles for city use. General Motors has placed its focus on the electric sports vehicle.

Car producers will respond to customers' market behavior and the policy signals given by governments. Without such signals – and the resulting competitive pressures – many otherwise worthy concept vehicles and sustainable transport systems will stay on the shelf.

Transport congestion hits industry as hard as the general public. If we try to pursue *mobility* with the current approach, there will never be enough road, rail or air space to satisfy everyone. But if, instead, we focus on *access*, we might find ourselves developing more sustainable solutions.

Some companies are experimenting with innovative logistics. Fiat, General Motors and Volkswagen are engaged in "intelligent" traffic-management and road systems – evidence that electronics is changing the automotive sector.

In Sweden, competing freight companies ASG[31] and BTL[32] offer "Green Return" and "Green Logistics" services for their customers. They recognize that increasing demands for re-use and recycling will place demands on transport systems, and they are working on "reverse logistics" services to bring materials or products back for remanufacturing or recycling.

But the most radical approach to reducing travel is likely to come from those who encourage us to communicate electronically rather than face-to-face. For example, British Telecom has said that its internal use of video-conferencing avoids the need for 6.6 million kilometers of travel.

Strategy Unit, Chairman's Office **sdx**

briefing note 00/02.09   February 2000

■ Waste

Waste is a double loss: we have to replace a valuable raw material lost in the production process and we are running out of places where we can dispose of our garbage. Moreover, hazardous waste is another important issue with strong emotional public overtones.

Accordingly, there is a common interest among producers, consumers and society at large to *reduce waste at the source*. This is the key to the cleaner production approach.

■ Policy responses

Today, the OECD countries are the main generators of **industrial waste**.

But while the "post-industrial revolution" will lead to more software-oriented and knowledge-oriented industries in the OECD, the developing countries – and especially the newly industrialized countries – will grow rapidly in the areas of traditional and raw-material-intensive industries.

In many developing countries, difficulties in gaining access to investment capital, lack of waste legislation by governments, and a growing population in need of products and services, will increase the waste problems. These countries were also in the past repositories for waste from industrialized nations, a practice that was halted by the Basel Convention, which restricts the transboundary movement of certain materials and includes a ban on the export of recyclable hazardous waste from OECD to non-OECD countries.

Until 20 years ago, governments showed little concern about **toxic waste**. This has changed

with the realization that old, uncontrolled landfills containing hazardous waste entail serious environmental risks. Furthermore, there has been a growing reluctance by the public to accept landfills or treatment plants for the disposal of hazardous waste – the so-called NIMBY (Not In My Back Yard) phenomenon.

An important objective of international policies after the Rio Summit is the international assessment of **chemical hazards**. The aim is to institute a worldwide system for classifying and labeling chemicals – both for safe transport and for use – and for providing information on all hazardous chemicals involved in international transactions.

■ Business challenges and opportunities

The production of goods and services without the concurrent production of residues and waste has long been regarded as an ideal, but has never been thought to be economically viable. Things are now beginning to change:

- The production of rapidly rising volumes of waste has forced a rethinking of the whole issue at a time when companies are focusing on improvements in production efficiency and looking for cost-cutting measures.

- Simple calculations of the market value of chemicals that have been flushed down the drain support the view that emissions, effluents and other residues, in addition to being pollutants, are in fact a wasted resource.

Waste minimization, pollution prevention and recycling are more and more being regarded as elements in an economic strategy to produce goods without waste.

We use the term **cleaner production** to describe a *preventative approach* to resource efficiency and the waste generated from industrial activities.

Industry in many countries is today working on cleaner production strategies, mainly driven by *competitive pressures to be more efficient*, but also to reduce *future liabilities and costs*.

This experience is shared through business organizations such as the WBCSD, the World Environment Center and the Global Environmental Management Initiative (GEMI) in the U.S., as well as through sectoral organizations. Industry is spreading its experiences through a partnership with the United Nations Environment Program (UNEP), an international driving force for cleaner production.

Waste minimization has therefore become very much part of management's task in many companies today and is a key to their remaining competitive – in the same way that quality became the watchword some decades ago.

The challenge for business in the future is how to integrate cleaner production with the other competitive requirements for the company of tomorrow.

Note: **For more on the Basel Convention, see Sections Three and Four . . .**

SECTION THREE

Policy Topics on Today's Board Agenda

> *The time to consider the policy dimensions of climate change is not when the link between greenhouse gases and climate change is conclusively proven, but when the possibility cannot be discounted and is taken seriously by the society of which we are part.*
>
> John Browne, CEO, British Petroleum

IN THIS SECTION we will focus on topics that are at the heart of ongoing debates.

▶ *The Climate Negotiations*

What are the issues and the options in the global warming debate? What is the impact of the 1997 Kyoto negotiations, and what about Joint Implementation and Tradable Permits?

▶ *The Biodiversity Convention*

How is the impact of the Biodiversity Convention felt by the business sector? We have invited the World Resources Institute, a leading policy analysis and research centre in the US, to outline the challenges for business.

▶ *Multilateral Environmental Agreements*

What other Multilateral Environmental Agreements will business have to deal with and know about? How will the Basel convention, CITES and other binding UN agreements influence international business?

▶ *The Food Challenge*

How can business contribute to meeting the international need for food? We have again asked the World Resources Institute to identify the key areas of concern and suggest how business could approach this challenge.

▶ *Sustainability and Business from a Southern View*

We must not forget that sustainable development is more than environmental protection or conservation. The last theme in this section therefore takes up the role of business in the development challenge of the poorer countries.

Carlo Novoponte
Chairman

To: Board Members
From: Carlo Novoponte
Date: March 2, 2000
Subject:

Key policy topics on the board agenda

I have asked the Government Relations Department to put together a file on international policy issues in preparation for next Monday's Board Meeting. These issues will directly affect SDX's operations in the years ahead. We need to have a clear strategy for dealing with them and I should like us to make a start on formulating this at our next board meeting.

One point on which I know we all agree is this: Business needs a long-term policy direction from governments in order to allocate its capital, technology and human resources efficiently. We have investment cycles of 20 years or more in our business sectors but in some other sectors those cycles are in excess of 40 years.

Governmental policies should therefore avoid the costly and premature retirement of capital. They should rather encourage business to invest in the developing world. Here, the rapid economic expansion of the developing world calls for "leap-frogging" to the latest technology.

I should therefore like us to round off our board debate with discussion of what our business strategy in developing countries should be — a subject covered in the last items in this file.

C.J. Novoponte

SDX Corporation, SDX Technology Park, Cambridge MA 10000
Tel: 617-000-1111   Fax: 617-000-1486   http://xyz.sdx.web

For attention of:
SDX Board Members
Briefing notes for Board Meeting
of 7th March, 2000

Prepared by
L. Benotti, Govt Relations

Government Relations Department

Board Briefing
March 2000

The Climate Negotiations

An Update for the Board of SDX Corporation

■ Introduction

The climate debate has been on the board agenda ever since the United Nations Convention on Climate Change was signed in Rio 1992 with the aim of stabilizing emissions of greenhouse gases at 1990 levels by the year 2000.

What is the issue?

- The natural greenhouse effect is being amplified by the release of a range of industrial and other greenhouse gases, including carbon dioxide (CO_2), methane (CH_4), nitrous oxide (N_2O) and CFCs.

- Greenhouse gases are being produced from a huge range of natural and people-controlled sources and from a bewildering spectrum of activities.

- The largest man-made contribution to greenhouse gases comes from CO_2, primarily from the combustion of fossil fuels.

- Deforestation destroys one of the major CO_2 sinks, and the burning of cut trees and vegetation releases CO_2 stored previously.

- CH_4, another important greenhouse gas, is emitted from rice cultivation, coal-mining, leakage from gas pipelines and releases from waste dumps.

- Sources of N_2O emissions include natural aerobic decomposition of organic matter, other bacterial processes, and from fossil fuel combustion and fertilizers.

Mathematical models of global climate patterns suggest that there may be a long-term temperature increase, leading to changes in climate patterns. But available data are not yet adequate to prove or disprove these predictions. If the predictions are correct – as an overwhelming majority of scientists believe they are – they may lead to:

- A rise in sea level (projected to be perhaps 0.5 meters by 2100)

- Increases in the frequency and severity of storms

- Shifts in ocean currents

- Extinction of species failing to adapt quickly enough

- Reductions in rainfall

- More rapid spread of some infectious diseases

■ The Framework Convention on Climate Change

The objective of this Convention is to address and ultimately prevent the impact of human conduct, in particular greenhouse gas emissions, on the global climate system. The original emissions requirement was a best-efforts commitment on developed countries to return to 1990 emission levels of greenhouse gases by 2000. 167 states are party to the Convention that came into force in 1992.

The Convention includes no trade measures at this time, but may do so at some point in the future, in particular to help enforce the agreement and to deter free riders.

The Convention has perhaps the broadest potential impacts of any international environmental agreement. It affects fossil-fuel-producing industries, heavy users of fossil fuels, transportation, home and office heating and cooling, agricultural activities, waste landfills, forestry, and other areas. Indeed, almost all aspects of modern life can be seen as potentially impacted to some extent over the life of the Convention.

In addition to agreeing binding emissions targets, the Convention approved at the 1997 Kyoto meeting a system of joint implementation of obligations between countries and tradable emissions permits in order to achieve greenhouse gas reductions through economic instruments as opposed to traditional regulatory ones. These approaches will mitigate some of the potential impacts on trade and competitiveness.

The results of the Second International Panel on Climate Change (IPCC) Assessment in 1996 confirmed earlier concerns about the likelihood of climate change caused by human activity. The follow-up IPCC report, due in 2001, will look more deeply into the mitigation of and adaptation to such climate changes. Industry is invited to play a major role in this report.

■ What is the business position?

Although there seems still to be some uncertainty over the magnitude, timing and effects of potential climate changes, business organizations such as the WBCSD have suggested that prudent action is warranted *now*. Business is now recognized as one of the key players and will be prominently integrated into the debate so that business's valuable experience is properly taken account of.

Climate change must be approached from a *global perspective* to ensure that goals can actually be achieved. Building an international government policy response has been difficult and the challenge has been intensified by uncertainty about the effects caused by the undoubted increase in greenhouse gas concentrations, and about the massive economic implications of the likely changes required.

The UN Convention on Climate Change is only a "framework" that sets out the major objectives and directions for reducing the amount of greenhouse gas in the atmosphere. However, through its binding **protocols** it aims to ensure that the objectives and goals are met.

64

THE SUSTAINABLE BUSINESS CHALLENGE

The *Conference of the Parties* (COP) negotiations are meetings among the governments that have signed and ratified the Convention, in order to agree on protocols on how the Convention should be implemented.

The message of business organizations such as the WBCSD has been to urge governments to strive for feasible targets and to focus on technology development and market-based mechanisms such as Joint Implementation and tradable permits.

■ The importance of the Kyoto Protocol

In December 1997, governments agreed in Kyoto to a Protocol that establishes a legally binding obligation on Annex B countries (most OECD countries and Central and Eastern Europe). The obligation is to reduce their emissions of a combination of six greenhouse gases, so that by the years 2000–2012 they are, on average, 5.2% below 1990's levels.

The Protocol provides significant flexibility: there are no mandatory policies and measures defining how to achieve the targets. Countries are allowed to adopt many ways and select those policies best suited to their economic circumstances.

Kyoto has moved the climate debate from a general policy debate to a concrete framework which businesses can relate to.

The Protocol firmly agreed to:

- Policy measures that are accountable in a budget period 2008–2012 and which allow for burden-sharing (so-called "bubbles," under which the emissions of European Union members, for example, are averaged out).

- Joint Implementation and Emission Trading among Annex B countries.

- A new instrument ("Clean Development Mechanism") that will allow developing countries to benefit from project activities that result in certified emission reductions. Under this mechanism, Annex B countries can sponsor projects and acquire a part of the emissions reductions these projects generate, and they can use them after 2000 as part of their compliance with targets.

The Kyoto Protocol postponed for later resolution several important questions of measurement, verification and institutional mechanisms.

But it's important to note that governments invited business to contribute to these discussions. SDX has clearly stated that it is interested in participating in the debate and in contributing to developing cost-effective solutions to these remaining challenges.

– 3

Before kyoto, the question was: "Does climate change exist?" After Kyoto, the debate is on: "How do we respond to climate change most effectively?"

CJN.

**World Business Council
for Sustainable Development**

Climate Change
Summary of the WBCSD's Recommendations for Action

▶ Scientific and economic research must continue so as to bring a better understanding of the environmental and economic effects of greenhouse gases.

▶ Research and technological development can improve the efficiency with which energy is used and new carbon-free energy technologies are developed.

▶ Government support can accelerate this process because inadequate market incentives and the long pay-back of such research seldom provide sufficient attraction for business.

▶ Governments should build policies on properly designed market-based approaches, eliminate counter-productive subsidies and establish incentives for exploring and promoting highly efficient technologies.

▶ GHG emissions can be reduced through:

- Demand-side energy-efficient technologies

- Reducing energy distribution losses

- Using renewable forms of energy and developing highly efficient energy conversion technologies and carbon-free energy sources

▶ In addition, there is much to be gained from exploiting and disseminating current technology that extracts maximum efficiency from conventional fuels and hardware, and from encouraging sequestration by sustainable forest management.

▶ Global implementation of the Convention is a high priority.

▶ It is important to develop economic incentives and reduce barriers to international technology transfer, joint implementation and emissions-reduction trading.

▶ These instruments will lower the cost of reducing emissions dramatically and are necessary to make GHG reductions cost-effective around the world.

The Environmental Partnership

29 rue de la Rotisserie
CH 1204 Geneva Switzerland
Tel 41 22 819 85 00
Fax 41 22 819 85 50

CompuServe
100341.2622

JFR/fr - sdx.doc

Geneva, February 25 2000

Mr Peter Kennedy
CEO
SDX Corporation
SDX Technology Park
Cambridge, MA 10000

Re: Joint Implementation and Carbon Trading

Dear Mr Kennedy

When we saw each other earlier this year in Davos, you asked me for a briefing on where Joint Implementation is today. And where it may go if carbon trading really takes off.

The first critical step linking Joint Implementation with trading was taken with the Kyoto Protocol in December 1997. Since then, many details have been worked out, including the procedures linking Joint Implementation with the new "clean mechanism". All these small and big steps amount to a slow but steady process of developing systems to give economic value to the services of nature.

Article 4 of the Climate Convention provides for the parties to meet their commitments to reduce GHG emissions "jointly with other parties". The original idea, as suggested already during the Rio meeting, is fairly straightforward: it allows a company that is generating greenhouse gases (or investors in a country that has commitments) to finance or participate in projects in other countries to reduce the net emission of GHG, and in return receive credits in their home country for some of the quantity of emissions reduced.

An example of Joint Implementation

A private power company (or maybe a public agency operating power plants) is required by law or pressed by international convention to cut its carbon emissions or at least keep them from increasing. If it is inconvenient or costly for the power company to do so in its own country, it may "purchase" reduction in some other country.

The power company (or public agency) might do this by building a non-emitting plant in Costa Rica, as the U.S.'s Northern Utilities has done with a 20-megawatt wind farm there. Or it might buy the equivalent of a conservation easement on a tract of Costa Rican forest, so that, rather than being converted to pastureland or some other non-forested state, the land is maintained in its natural state as a capturer ("sequesterer") of carbon. Or it might simply pay for reforestation.

This system creates a "market in virtue" and, in theory at least, brings about pollution reduction at the lowest possible cost.[33]

EPS
Environmental Services SA

During the pilot phase of JI (where JI was called "Activities Implemented Jointly" - or AIJ) no carbon credits were given under the Climate Convention, but from 2000 on, some form of carbon-crediting is allowed, at least among Annex B countries (OECD and Central and Eastern European countries, except Turkey).

Initial AIJ projects were launched within Annex B countries, involving Central and Eastern European countries, where there are many opportunities to reduce GHG emissions under such a joint programme, and with Costa Rica.[33]

What are the benefits? For investors like yourselves, JI provides an opportunity to meet commitment by financing foreign projects that reduce GHG emissions at a lower cost than the domestic options. As the climate issue is a global problem, the value of reducing GHG emissions in one country is as valuable for the environment as doing it in another country. Like in international trade, investments should flow to where they find the biggest return.

The link to emission trading

For the partners in the country in which an investment is being made, JI provides that host country with technology, experience and financing of projects. It also generates a new economic value, the carbon credit, which is initially owned by the host country: It may decide to retain all or part of that value, or compensate the foreign investors with part of the carbon offset for their investment and technology provided.

The value of such carbon offsets would increase if there was a real international market. JI projects will therefore only become the important technology co-operation tool once carbon offset trading picks up on an international scale. Then, the emission credits produced by any JI projects would become a commodity just as, for example, copper is a commodity. There is a market for copper because firms are willing to pay for it. Similarly, there would be a market for emission credits because investor countries' commitment to limit their GHG emissions lead them to require that their firms limit their emissions. Credits would be used by these firms together with land, labour, capital and materials as factors of production in, for example, generating electricity. And just as a country with copper resources might seek a foreign investor in a mining project, so too might a host partner join with a foreign partner and investor in a JI project. In each case, the host country has a comparative advantage in producing the commodity (copper or credits), at a low cost, and exports it another country in exchange for something it values more highly.[34]

In summary, if JI investment generates an asset in the form of a carbon offset potential, its value is only real if someone wants to have it, i.e. if there is a market for it. The World Bank has created such a market with their Carbon Offset Fund, and I suggest therefore that you should participate in this effort.

Setting up a Carbon Offset Fund

The development of GHG emission trading - or the likelihood that such a market will exist in the near future - thus becomes a strong incentive for developing JI further. But it always takes someone to take the first steps and be "market-maker".

Norway in a way served as such a market-maker by purchasing Costa Rican Certified Tradable Offsets (CTOs) for $4 million in 1997, thereby setting a price in the market. This sent a strong signal to others that there was a belief in this market in the future. The World Bank in parallel took the initiative to bring those companies and countries together to explore how one could build a Carbon Offset Fund. The objective is to attract the capital that would be required to finance the additional cost of projects that generate carbon offsets at a reasonable price. The likelihood for generating good CTOs through the projects in which the World Bank is already involved (and thus knows the commercial risks of) should compensate for the political uncertainties we still have of getting a tradable regime for approved JI projects operational.

The Costa Rican Government has taken a first step and offered in May 1997 greenhouse gas emission mitigation certificates, thus encouraging the development of a market. Each of the initial 4 million Certifiable Tradable Offsets (CTOs) represents the halted or reduced emission into the atmosphere of one metric tonne of carbon.

The credibility of the CTOs will be ensured by an independent certification process developed with technical assistance from the World Bank. The Costa Rican Office for Joint Implementation has worked with WBCSD member SGS to certify the offsets and provide continuous monitoring of compliance.

The Costa Rica Example

The Costa Rican financial instrument allows one to invest in pollution reduction through a type of bond that will eventually be tradable on commodity markets. It provides funds for the consolidation of the National Parks and biological reserves of the country through reforestation or forest protection. This approach also permits generation of multiple income streams from the same tract of forest by activities that don't affect carbon storage, such as eco-tourism or extraction of minor forest products. The combined revenues constitute a powerful alternative to deforestation.[35]

UNCTAD, UNEP, Centre Financial Products Ltd of the Chicago Board of Trade and the Earth Council are completing the process to launch a pilot trading system for those FCCC parties that have committed themselves to quantitative GHG emissions limitations, and are exploring with the FCCC different models:

- Under an <u>Allowance Trading System</u>, the agreement would establish an overall group net emission cap, an allocation of net emissions allowances among the members, and institutional arrangements for trading allowances, monitoring and imposing sanctions for non-compliance.

- Under an <u>Emission Budget System</u>, members would commit themselves to limiting cumulative emissions during each of several successive multi-year budget periods. A member's reductions of emissions below the amount budgeted for a given period would generate savings that could be reserved for future use or traded.

The objective is to make a trading system fully operational by 2001.

I am certain that there are interesting opportunities for SDX to play a leading role in these developments and benefit from their business opportunities.

Best regards

Juan F. Rada
Managing Director

WORLD RESOURCES INSTITUTE

The Challenge of Biodiversity

As viewed by the World Resources Institute

EARTH IS HOME to a wide variety of plants, animals and other living things. Most birds, mammals and plants have been identified. Little is known, however, about other orders, such as insects, or about organisms that inhabit poorly explored habitats, such as the deep-sea floor. The current total of all identified species is about 1.7 million. However, this number pales next to estimates of the total number of species, which has been put conservatively at close to 14 million by an international group of experts (but could range from 3 million to 111 million species). Much of this wide range is accounted for by insects, which could number anywhere from 2 million to 100 million species; the working estimate is 8 million species.[36]

Many of the world's species are gravely threatened. Various projections suggest that from 1975 to 2015 between 1 and 11% of the world's species per decade will become extinct. The three most important causes include habitat loss, species introductions (accidental and deliberate), and the hunting of species for food or for wildlife trade. In fact, trading in illegal wildlife is second only to illicit narcotics (in dollar value) in the illegal trade economy.

Such losses impose profound costs at both a practical and intangible level. Species diversity provides a host of wild and domestic plant, fish and animal products used for medicines, cosmetics, industrial products, fuel and building materials, and food, among other things. Species diversity also plays a vital role in the functioning of ecosystems.

Biodiversity: why it is important

Biodiversity benefits the world in three general manners: a practical manner, an ecological manner and an aesthetic manner. Practical value can be attached to biodiversity at various levels in providing for human needs. Biodiversity helps provide for genetic diversity among a population of a species. In corn crops, for instance, genetic diversity has promoted unique characteristics of some corn populations and has left them resistant to certain pests. Farmers can select for these traits when faced with infestations, rather than resigning themselves to heavy pesticide use or high crop loss. Furthermore, one-quarter of pharmaceuticals dispensed in the United States contains active ingredients derived from plant products. New medicinal plants, as well as new food sources adapted to difficult climate and soil conditions, may improve the health and living standards of growing human populations around the world.

Biodiversity is also important for healthy ecosystems, which are subsequently crucial for humans because of the goods and services they provide, such as recycling water, gas, nutrients and other materials. Wetlands, for example, ameliorate water flow resulting from rainfall, filtering sediments in the process. In total, the value of the world's ecological functions, such as recycling water and gas, has been estimated at U.S.$33 *trillion* per year (global GNP is estimated at U.S.$18 trillion per year).[37] Along with its natural functions, biodiversity is valued by many people for the recreational and intangible benefits that wildlife and wild areas offer.

Threats to biodiversity

If the benefits of biodiversity are not realized and addressed by the world soon, grave consequences may result. By some accounts, the world is on the verge of an episode of major species extinction, perhaps rivalling five other documented periods over the past half billion years during which a significant portion of global fauna and flora were wiped out. The most recent event occurred 65 million years ago when the dinosaurs disappeared. Experts suggest that, following each extinction period, it took 10 million years or more for the number of species to return to the level of diversity existing prior to the event in question.

Unlike previous die-offs, for which climatic, geologic and other natural phenomena were to blame, experts say the current episode is driven by anthropogenic factors. A World Conservation Union analysis of animal extinctions since 1600 found that, where the cause was known, 39% had resulted from species introductions, 36% from habitat destruction, and 23% from hunting and deliberate extermination. While the analysis focuses on island species, it is generally agreed that these factors, particularly species introduction and habitat loss, are major threats to biodiversity everywhere. When pollution is added to the assortment of dangers, the threats to biodiversity become more difficult to overcome.

If these warnings prove true, the effect of human activities on biodiversity — the variation of genes within a species and the overall diversity of species, communities and ecosystems — will be irreparable if continued unchecked, within the time-frame of subsequent generations.

SOLUTIONS

New biodiversity assessment

Having an accurate assessment of the problem at hand begins the solution process. In 1995, UNEP released its *Global Biodiversity Assessment* report, which detailed strategies to protect biodiversity. The traditional approach to protecting biodiversity emphasized the separation of ecosystems, species and genetic resources from human activity through the creation of protected areas, prohibitions on harvesting endangered species, and the preservation of germ plasm in seed banks or cryogenic storage facilities. Scientists now think that it is impossible to shield all genes, species and ecosystems from human influence. The earlier focus had been on conservation; the new focus is on conservation and enhancing biodiversity within human-dominated areas. Preservation efforts must include programs to save species by recreating environments and controlling them to aid the species who thrive there, and policies to manage natural environments in ways that minimize adverse impacts on biodiversity.

Protecting biodiversity

There are two management-level approaches to biodiversity conservation: protecting individual species and populations, and protecting the habitats they live in. Efforts directed at species and populations, while important, are time- and resource-intensive and thus can only support a small percentage of threatened species. Measures include offering legal protection to individual species, developing management plans targeted at protecting them in their natural habitat (in situ conservation), and ex situ conservation, that is, protecting animal and plant populations in zoos and seed banks. Ex situ conservation serves as insurance against the loss of genetic and species diversity in the wild, a source for occasional releases to reintroduce or bolster wild populations, and as a source of genetic diversity for agricultural research. Some zoos and NGOs have shifted resources towards in situ conservation, which has proven more efficient with resources and more effective at preserving large numbers of species.

Policy-makers and managers are expanding the network of parks and reserves and redefining the protected-area concept to better accommodate humans and safeguard biodiversity. They are also expanding the management scale to consider biodiversity at the landscape and at the corridor levels. Landscape biodiversity consists of the matrix of habitats located on settled and undeveloped lands. Biodiversity corridors link together protected or pristine areas (of which many have been cut and intruded upon by human development) and are used by species that need large tracts of land to survive. These corridors also prevent a species population from becoming isolated and interbreeding, which can cause extinction.

Facing scarce financial resources, policy-makers and managers are increasingly turning to private and community groups for support of expansion and management. Integrated conservation development projects (ICDPs) represent a new management approach that seeks to reduce human impact on protected areas by providing local populations with sustainable, income-generating opportunities. Many ICDPs are far-reaching, managing protected areas within the context of the surrounding landscape. The broad variety of ICDPs range from community development initiatives in areas bordering parks to regional land-use planning targeted at protected areas and surrounding lands.[38] Biosphere reserves are well-known examples, although only some are managed with both conservation and development in mind.[39] These reserves consist of protected core areas, often existing parks, surrounded by buffer zones and transition areas where some human activity is permitted. The biosphere model offers local people economic opportunity through the sustainable management of resources in non-core areas of the reserve, while extending the total area managed for biodiversity beyond core boundaries.

In many cases, governments lack the staff or financial resources to manage an existing network of protected areas, much less to invest in the creation of new reserves. One solution is to work with private and non-governmental organizations (NGOs). Private groups can raise money to purchase land for protection and to support conservation in existing parks. They are often in a better position than government agencies to negotiate land-use disputes and to incorporate local interests in management decisions. In some Latin American countries, including Belize, El Salvador and Ecuador, NGO and community groups currently manage protected areas.

Bioregional management, conducted at the landscape and corridor levels as part of other land-management efforts, allows for biodiversity conservation at all levels, from maintaining ecosystem function to preserving genetic diversity within individual populations. Only by managing entire watersheds can hydrological cycles be maintained or the habitat needs of broad-ranging and freshwater species be accounted for.

World Business Council
for Sustainable Development

How the Convention on Biological Diversity touches various industries

A summary by the WBCSD

Pharmaceutical	A key issue for the pharmaceutical sector is to develop agreements for **Intellectual Property Rights** (IPRs), which simultaneously satisfy developing-country concerns with respect to the equitable sharing of benefits while also meeting the industry's patent concerns. Other issues include the transfer of pharmacological expertise in **bioprospecting**; the transfer of results from research and development to local communities and indigenous people to address issues of **sharing of benefits.**
Agricultural/Seed	**Biosafety guidelines** are being developed at international and national levels to control the safety of the trade in genetically modified organisms. These guidelines will most likely become part of a protocol to the Convention.
Petroleum	The petroleum sector can expect future restrictions on **access** to land, marine and coastal areas; the possible **limitation of transport routes** as a result of more detailed environmental impact assessments (EIAs); more stringent requirements for ecosystem **monitoring**; and greater **participation** by local communities and indigenous peoples, e.g. with respect to technology-transfer and equitable-sharing issues.
Mining	The mining sector will also have to face future restrictions on access to land because of more detailed EIAs. Other issues include the need for mining companies to develop **biodiversity policies** and include greater participation of local communities and indigenous peoples in order to address issues of **equity sharing. Biosafety** could also become an issue as a result of the use of biological metallurgical processes to remove gold and other minerals from ore.
Fisheries	The institutional framework of the fisheries industry, including common access and subsidized fleets, is now being seriously questioned.
Retail	Retailers will increasingly request confirmation from producers that their products have been produced in a "biodiversity-friendly" manner.
Banking	The banking sectors will increasingly be looking to fund new "biodiversity-friendly" projects.
Energy	The hydro-electricity industry will be particularly concerned with preserving biodiversity and reducing the impact of its operations on the biodiversity of the large areas of land and water it manages.
Manufacturing	The main biodiversity issues will vary depending on the location and the product and process of manufacture. For example, in developing countries, technology transfer will be an important consideration.
Forestry	The principal issue in the forestry sector is to ensure sustainable forestry management, including the conservation of biodiversity, through the use of adaptive forestry practices. Other issues include requirements for more detailed EIAs and ecosystem monitoring, and participation of local communities and indigenous people.

**World Business Council
for Sustainable Development**

Other Multilateral Environmental Agreements

What are Multilateral Environmental Agreements and why are they important to business?

An overview compiled by Margaret Flaherty, WBCSD

MULTILATERAL ENVIRONMENTAL AGREEMENTS (MEAs) are international treaties negotiated by states to address environmental concerns that affect more than one country. These can be negotiated bilaterally, regionally or globally. At present, there are several hundred such agreements in place. However, only a few of them include measures that directly regulate trade in the substances, material or wildlife regulated by the agreement, and fewer still have a significant impact on trade.

While some agreements may raise trade concerns for specific sectors, only five current MEAs and two agreements under negotiation are of broad concern in relation to trade. These selected agreements are noted in the following pages, which are designed to give an overview of the subject of the agreement, the trade measure used and the reason for it, possible trade impacts of the MEA, and the current state of play as regards the business-related issues raised by the agreement.

We will therefore look into the most important MEAs, besides the Framework Convention on Climate Change and the Biodiversity Convention:

◆ *The Basel Convention*
◆ *Trade in Chemicals: Prior Informed Consent*
◆ *The Montreal Protocol*
◆ *Trade in Endangered Species*

Basel Convention on the Control of Transboundary Movements of Hazardous Wastes and their Disposal

Purpose

To control the transboundary movement of hazardous wastes for final disposal and recycling. Basel was developed primarily but not exclusively in response to concerns of developing countries that hazardous waste from developed countries was increasingly being dumped in the developing world.

The Convention originally included a well-defined prior informed consent procedure that required a state of export to have the consent of the state of import prior to any trans-border movements commencing. The state of export also had to be convinced the wastes would be handled in an environmentally sound manner in the state of import before authorizing the movement. In addition, states party to Basel were prohibited from having any waste trades with non-parties unless a bilateral agreement requiring environmentally sound management was in place. State parties were also given the right to ban the import or export of any hazardous waste in the exercise of its national sovereignty.

In September 1995, the Conference of the Parties adopted an amendment to the Convention that will, when it comes into force, ban the trade in hazardous wastes from developed to developing countries for both final disposal and recycling. Since then, the parties have been reviewing the list of wastes covered by the Convention.

Impact on business

The Convention impacts industries involved in waste management, waste and co-product generators, recycling, scrap metal traders, and others. Industry groups opposed the ban amendment, and remain very concerned that it will be used for trade protectionist purposes rather than legitimate environmental ones. Some of these concerns may be alleviated when the review of the covered wastes is completed. There is also serious concern that the ban will unnecessarily limit valuable trade in secondary resources to developing countries, at their expense. As a result, some more technologically advanced developing countries are seeking to be placed on the Parties list that will allow them to engage in trade of recyclables with developed countries.

This is important for SDX!!

CJN.

The future

The Basel Convention history shows the ability of a regime to move from controls to full prohibitions in a short period of time. It is the most controversial example of the use of trade measures in environmental agreements. Significant debate is still anticipated as the implementation of the trade ban begins. The parties also continue to work on a Protocol on Liability and Compensation for damages resulting from the transboundary movement of hazardous wastes. Such a protocol may alter the costs for transboundary movements, including for recycling, and impact trade as a result.

Prior Informed Consent for Trade in Hazardous Chemicals

Purpose

To protect the environment and human health in a receiving state by regulating the export of a chemical or chemical product from a state where its use is banned or severely restricted, and its import into the receiving jurisdiction.

The basic tool of the agreement will be a prior informed consent (PIC) procedure for the trade in hazardous chemicals, understood as those chemicals banned or severely restricted in the country of manufacture. The emphasis in the negotiations is on the exchange of information to ensure informed decisions on imports or exports of such chemicals. Two existing international instruments already provide PIC requirements for industrial and agricultural chemicals, but are non-binding in nature. These are the UNEP London Guidelines and the FAO Code of Conduct, both from 1979. There is also a 1994 voluntary Code of Ethics on the International Trade in Chemicals.

Impact on business

The scope of the negotiations are generally within the scope of what is already included in the UNEP and FAO instruments. These already reach many chemical manufacturers, certain product manufacturers and pesticide manufacturers. In addition to requiring the prior informed consent procedure to be followed, similar labeling requirements, product information and use instructions, packaging requirements, etc. will also be included. Although the existing international agreements are non-binding in nature, some states and the EU have adopted legislation to implement their provisions. The legal nature of the new agreement will mean a greater number of countries passing PIC legislation, and probably on a broader range of products.

The future

Check with London office CJN.

The negotiations are proceeding under the auspices of UNEP and the FAO, and the regime is being designed to allow the initial steps already taken to regulate the international trade in chemicals to become legally binding. Additional steps may be contemplated later, if needed. If the regime is not widely adopted, or is seen to be too weak to protect recipient countries, most notably developing countries, international pressure for a ban on trade in banned or restricted chemicals may grow. This creates some parallels to the Basel Convention issues and approaches.

In addition, producers of chemicals, pesticides and industrial wastes that are classified as persistent organic pollutants (POPs) may also be impacted by negotiations that are taking place in the regional forum of the UN Economic Commission for Europe. POPs include both industrial and agricultural chemicals.

Montreal Protocol on Substances that Deplete the Ozone Layer

Purpose

To prevent the continuing depletion of the ozone layer that surrounds the planet and protects it from harmful ultra-violet rays, the Ozone Protocol included phase-outs and bans on ozone-depleting substances. To ensure a broad application of these requirements, incentives for developing-country participation were included. The Protocol celebrated its tenth anniversary in 1999, having come into force in 1989; 161 governments are party to the Protocol.

The Protocol includes a prohibition on trade with non-parties, and a phase-out on production and trade between the parties, of ozone-depleting substances or products containing them. This Protocol was the first major environmental agreement dealing with emissions or wastes, as opposed to wildlife protection, to include significant trade measures. Since its inception, the Protocol has expanded its original coverage from CFCs to other ozone-depleting substances such as halons, carbon tetrachloride and methyl bromide.

Trade measures were included in order to prevent international production processes from shifting from one country to another, and thereby frustrating the purpose of the Protocol. They were also designed to meet the recognition that all countries had to participate to achieve the environmental goal. In the face of a growing international black-market trade in CFCs, a mechanism has been developed in order to better monitor and enforce compliance and implementation by all parties.

A state that meets the environmental requirements of the Protocol but is not a party to it can seek a decision of the Convention that it be allowed to trade with the parties as if it were a member.

Impacts on business

The Protocol covers a wide range of different industries, from electronics to refrigeration, and others. As additional substances are added to the list of regulated or prohibited ozone-depleting substances, the range of industry potentially impacted will grow. The inclusion of most countries in the regime and the growing use of alternative technologies has eased competitiveness concerns. A co-operative industry structure has also helped ease implementation.

While the trade measures were considered something of a surprise when concluded, they do not appear to cause any significant controversy today. They have been repeated for new substances that have been added to the phase-outs and prohibitions under the Protocol.

Convention on International Trade in Endangered Species (CITES)

Purpose

To protect wildlife, both flora and fauna, that are designated as endangered under the Conventions procedures. CITES has been best known for its steps to protect wild animals from extinction, in particular ivory-bearing animals. 132 countries have signed the Convention, which came into force in 1975

CITES was the first very broadly accepted environmental agreement to include trade measures. These included prohibitions on the trade in live animals or parts of animals that are endangered. This was designed to remove the profit brought by the international trade that lies at the root of the demand for rare wild flora and fauna. A special and limited trading regime for African ivory originating in designated countries and going to Japan was agreed to at the last Conference of the Parties, indicating the ability to adjust the regime in accordance with environmental requirements.

Impacts on business

With its restricted target of endangered species, CITES has not had a major impact on industrial relationships.

WORLD RESOURCES INSTITUTE

The Food Challenge

As viewed by the World Resources Institute[40]

DISCUSSIONS ABOUT the future of global agriculture take place in an unusual context: production is generally growing and is likely to continue to grow but, globally, the rate of growth is slowing. At the same time, nearly 90 million people are being added to the world's population every year, putting more pressure on the world's food production system.

In the face of these declining growth rates, many experts are concerned about the capacity of the world agricultural system to continue to increase production over the coming decades to feed an ever-larger world population. Other experts worry not so much about the growth potential of global production as they do about the poorest countries of Africa and Asia and the continuing prevalence of chronic under-nutrition in those regions. A further concern is whether there are ways to increase production while at the same time reducing environmental and resource damage.

Differences among regions and between rich and poor are an important subplot to this story. In two regions, sub-Saharan Africa and South Asia, food security and undernutrition problems seem relatively intractable. In both regions, population growth is still relatively high and poverty is persistent. Recent production trends in the most vulnerable developing countries do not seem noticeably worse than they were in the late 1960s and early 1970s. They remain, however, grossly inadequate to meet the needs of the current and future populations in those nations and to help generate the additional income among the poor necessary to reduce chronic undernutrition.

Can global production keep up?

Most studies agree that the key issues surrounding the growth of global food production include the potential for expanding cropland area and irrigated cropland area, for increasing yields, and for improving efficiency. Other scholars emphasize the importance of resource conservation and alternative production models that are less environmentally damaging than the conventional high-input approach.

Most studies indicate that, over the next few decades, global food production can continue to increase to meet "effective" demand, that is, the level of demand that corresponds to purchasing power, irrespective of food needs. This is not likely to be the case in sub-Saharan Africa and South Asia, however. These regions are likely to experience regional production shortages, food distribution problems and famines, as they do today. In addition, given the millions of people who lack the money to buy all the food they need, it is even more doubtful that growth in purchasing power will be adequate to raise per capita food consumption enough to eliminate undernutrition. In fact, the UN Food and Agriculture Organization (FAO) projects that, in 2010, some 30% of the population of sub-Saharan Africa will remain malnourished.

Growing more cereals in the United States or in other developed countries will not meet the food needs of the poor in developing countries. To improve the food security of this group, ways must be found to help farmers grow more of their own food. Many of these nations remain primarily rural and heavily dependent on the agricultural economy. Boosting domestic food production would thus be doubly positive, increasing both food supplies and the incomes of many of the poor.

RAISING FUTURE FOOD PRODUCTION

Increasing world agriculture production will depend on trends in six key areas: expanding cropland, expanding irrigation, increasing yields, minimizing soil degradation, improving the efficiency of water use, and reducing post-harvest losses.

Expanding cropland

The FAO estimates that, by 2010, the 760 million hectares of land currently in crop production in developing countries (excluding China) could increase by 12% to 850 million hectares. Of these 850 million hectares, 720 million hectares could be harvested in a given year — an increase of about 21% — because of greater cropping intensities.

Some experts believe that the potential for further expansion of cropland area is rapidly disappearing in most regions because of many factors. For one, bringing more hectares into cultivation usually has very high environmental costs, since nearly all cropland expansion involves converting forests, rangelands or other important habitat. In addition, the costs of developing infrastructure in remote areas is often prohibitively high. Furthermore, undeveloped areas usually are not prime cropland, so yields will generally be less than average.

Expanding irrigation

Irrigated land accounted for more than 50% of the increase in global food production from the mid-1960s to the mid-1980s and currently accounts for about one-third of total production. Irrigation promotes higher crop yields and, in many areas, also allows more than one crop per year, which dramatically increases production.

The FAO predicts that irrigated land in developing countries (excluding China) will expand at a rate of 0.8% annually, which is much slower than the 2.2% annual increase experienced during the 1970s and the 1.9% annual increase in the 1980s. Even with this slower growth rate, more than half of the increment in crop production between now and 2010 will come from irrigated land, according to the FAO model.

The rate at which cropland is brought under irrigation is declining, mainly because of the increasing cost of irrigation (both development and maintenance), the growing competition for water uses, and the decline in prices paid to farmers for the crops they raise. Irrigation's environmental and health impacts also may inhibit further expansion. Salinization and waterlogging problems from improper irrigation techniques reduce crop yields, constraining future gains in production. Furthermore, the extension of irrigation systems can lead to an increase in water-related diseases such as malaria or schistosomiasis in some regions by providing habitat for mosquitoes and other disease vectors.

Increasing yields

Yields of maize, rice, and wheat doubled between 1961 and 1991 in developing countries as a whole. From 1990 to 2010, cereal yields in developing countries (excluding China) are projected to increase by about 1.4% per year, according to the FAO. (This does not include increases due to greater cropping intensity.)

Although the FAO predicts that, on average, increased yields will contribute about 66% to future crop production growth, they project that yield increases will make the strongest contribution in South Asia (82%) and much smaller contributions in Latin America and Africa (53%).

Sceptics argue that the dramatic gains in yields achieved over the past three decades are not likely to be repeated, since more and more of the world's farmers are already using varieties with the highest genetic yield potential. Furthermore, they note that rice yields at experiment stations in Asia have been stagnant for many years.

Minimizing soil degradation

Faulty agricultural practices account for 28% of the world's degraded soils, including about one-quarter of the degraded soils in Africa and Asia and nearly two-thirds of the degraded soils in North America. Causes include shortening of the fallow period during shifting cultivation (shifting cultivation is the clearing of land — usually by fire — followed by phases of cultivation and a fallow period), cultivating hillsides without adequate erosion control measures, leaving soil exposed during fallow periods, and insufficient drainage of irrigation water. Overgrazing by livestock is another significant cause of land degradation, accounting for nearly half of all land degradation in Africa. The impact of soil degradation on production is difficult to determine.

In Africa and South Asia, inputs such as fertilizer have been used more sparsely, so the relative impact of degradation seems to be greater. One promising new development is the United Nations Convention to Combat Desertification, which could provide some new impetus for the management of croplands in the dry-land areas of Africa. The Convention calls for the development of national action programs that encourage diversification in agriculture, promote the use of drought-resistant crops and the application of integrated dry-land farming systems, and ensure the more integrated and sustainable management of agricultural and pastoral lands.

Improving the efficiency of water use

More efficient use of water in agriculture could result in expansion of the area of irrigated cropland or an increase in crop yields, or both. Such gains, however, will require significant investments in both infrastructure and institutional reform and can depend on crucial investments in agricultural education. More expensive irrigation improvements include pressurized systems, portable sprinklers, center pivots, moving lines, and drip systems.

With the many constraints that limit the expansion of irrigation, improvements to rain-fed cropland are important to future food production, for this category comprises 84% of total cropped land. There are many opportunities in this area: for example, techniques that increase soil moisture around the root zone can improve yields and reduce production risks.

Reducing post-harvest losses

Gains can be obtained through better processing and improved storage and distribution facilities (including roads and transport facilities). Improved food storage facilities may also reduce vulnerability to famines and food shortages. In developing countries, seemingly minor changes in handling crops, such as cereals, could result in significant reductions in post-harvest losses. For example, a simple fence may be all that is required to prevent further crop losses caused by pests, such as rodents. However, the cost of maintenance and/or replacement of such a device may outweigh the profit from this form of crop protection, especially for smaller, poorer farmers.

S O L U T I O N S

The International Food Policy Research Institute (IFPRI) has concluded that sustained action is needed to:

❏ Strengthen the capacities of developing-country governments to perform their appropriate functions.

❏ Enhance the productivity, health and nutrition of low-income people and increase their access to employment and productive assets.

❏ Strengthen agricultural research and extension systems in and for developing countries.

❏ Promote sustainable agricultural intensification and sound management of natural resources, with increased emphasis on areas with fragile soils, limited rainfall and widespread poverty.

❏ Develop effective, efficient and low-cost agricultural input and output markets.

❏ Expand international assistance and improve its efficiency. IFPRI recommends realigning international development assistance to low-income developing countries, primarily in sub-Saharan Africa and South Asia.

The Developing Country Dimension

Intergovernmental Panel on Industry

1 Industry Plaza, New York, NY 99999   Tel: 999 1119999   Fax: 999 2229999   http://xyz.ipi.web

BRIEFING NOTE

Date: **02-24-2000**

Re: **Private Capital Flow to Developing Countries:**
             The Role of Governments

Recent studies by UNCTAD, the World Bank and the IMF confirm that public-sector investments through international financial institutions are now a minor part of capital flow to environmental and developmental causes. Private capital investments in developing countries and countries in transition have been steadily growing. In 1990 these were estimated at U.S.$57 billion. They had reached U.S.$195 billion in 1995. This trend is causing concern among members for two reasons. Firstly, that these investments are likely to be going to *end-of-pipe* rather than cleaner production or eco-efficiency initiatives. Secondly, there is concern that this is indicative of a changing and weakening role and influence of government in environmental management as resources are bypassing them.

This situation is compounded by the move by many countries in recent years towards more democratic forms of government. The implication of this is that long-term sustainable development horizons will become subservient to the political imperative of the next election, particularly in developing countries where environmental policies and systems are often in their infancy. In many of these countries, the Ministry of the Environment is among the weakest elements of government. Their lead role in changing the mindset within government is thus particularly difficult. This is especially true when it comes to challenging more powerful colleagues – for example, on measures such as removing environmentally inappropriate subsidies.

What is the Future Role of Governments?

We have listed below some of the important roles that we see government as maintaining and developing.

1.   Contrary to some commentators' views, we believe that governments' role is not diminishing but the need for them to take a more aggressive leadership role is

increasing. In a rapidly "globalizing world" in which the power-base is shifting from government to business, the need is not only for responsible corporate governance from business but also for innovative ways of granting the social license to operate by government.

2. Only government can provide a negotiating forum, free from vested interests, enabling all stakeholders to develop a shared vision and locally relevant interpretation of the goal of a sustainable future for their territories. Too often public-sector technicians develop this vision unilaterally.

3. Consequently the corridors of government are replete with volumes of national policies and strategies that fail to be implemented. A sense of ownership shared among diverse stakeholders, and a negotiated policy, has far greater chance of success.

4. Once in place, the government role of tracking and reporting on the progress towards this goal against performance indicators and targets becomes crucial. These help to make the goals clearer and more consistent.

Negotiating a national position on evolving international agreements, protocols, conventions, etc. and then implementing the requirements nationally is of course crucial to us. Business input is essential to these national teams but only government can legitimately take the leadership position. They too will have the responsibility to translate global strategies into national action.

The search for new instruments of policy has never been more intense. Governments are well positioned to influence behavioral changes, particularly consumption and production behavior in the marketplace. Government decision-making affects taxes and resource subsidies (fossil fuel use, transport, electricity, water, farming practices, etc.), property rights, trade and market access, permitting, etc.

Governments' role in environmental management is therefore increasing.

It may even be entering a new stage. Not unlike the experiences in industry, the need was first to establish environmental expertise in an Environmental Department or Ministry; this was followed by the introduction of an environmental management system and then – and this is probably the stage many governments are now entering – the responsibility for environmental management fell to the "line function": whether in government or business, the situation is the same.

This is a recognition that environment is everyone's business and not a specialist activity on the periphery but deeply imbedded in every relevant activity. We should not therefore be alarmed by the higher profile business is gradually adopting *vis-à-vis* governments. Business, after all, has a principle responsibility and duty in environmental management and government must provide both the carrots and the sticks to ensure that it fulfils these responsibilities.

A View from Latin America

**World Business Council
for Sustainable Development**

Latin American Office

Peter Kennedy
CEO
SDX Corporation
SDX Technology Park
Cambridge, MA 10000

Nueva Léon, Mexico   February 18th, 2000

When searching for a sustainable pattern for development in emerging economies, education and training emerge as a clear and visible priority for any serious project. Sustainable development is more than just economic growth and generation of wealth; it transcends environmental protection. In practice, it is impossible to imagine that genuine development can be achieved without the eradication of poverty, the most appropriate administration of natural resources, and investment in human resources.

Education and training are the best-known and most efficient tools for use in undertaking the aforementioned tasks. Experience has shown that education is the safest mechanism to promote vertical social mobility and greater equality in any society. In like manner, an educated society is more conscious of the impact that its actions have on the environment and natural resources. Conversely, training and skill development are mechanisms that guarantee higher levels of labor productivity, which in turn are directly linked to higher levels of competitiveness, and ultimately to the economic growth of developing regions.

The recent Ibero American Conference on Education[41] in Venezuela concluded that education should be taken up by Latin America as a fundamental factor in the struggle against economic and technological backwardness. The underdevelopment of this region is evident. Given its level of income, the region's average scholastic attendance should be 7.2 years; the real level observed, however, is only five years of education. In fact, this education deficit has only risen in the last 20 years. Latin America's illiteracy rate is 81% for women and 85% for men respectively. The United Nations Children's Fund (UNICEF) indicates that, between 1986 and 1991, 94% of children in developed countries completed elementary education. In contrast, only 48% of Latin America's children had finished primary school in the same period. Recommendations of UNESCO (United Nations Education Science and Culture Organization) for Latin America and the Caribbean have established that public investment in education should be no less than 6.5% of Gross Domestic Product; currently this kind of investment in Latin America is a paltry 4.2%.

1/...3

This phenomenon is accentuated by the significant disharmony that exists in Latin America between commercial liberalization and structural reforms of, among other things, education, labor relations and best technology use. A report from the World Trade Organization (WTO) surmised that, while Latin American economies are recovering quickly from crisis, low-paying jobs account for most of the new growth in employment; eight in every ten new jobs are low paying, while more than half of the region's workforce continues to labor in the underground economy. The future economic success of developing countries depends enormously on education; reports from the International Institute for Management Development and the World Economic Forum identify a direct relationship between the productivity and competitiveness of countries and their education systems.

For their part, companies in developing countries must generate profits in an environment of instability, survive in an increasingly competitive market, and promote economic development in the region, while facing up to their social and environmental responsibilities. Following the Global Conference on Social Issues in Copenhagen, organized by the United Nations Program for Development (UNPD) in 1995, emphasis was placed on the social and environmental responsibility of business as a vital element for the survival of organizations in developing countries, where necessary framework conditions are lacking to guarantee the well-being of the population. Education and training to promote the integration of environmental and social considerations in the decision-making of companies is an unavoidable requisite.

In light of economic and technological change, workers must now possess a more solid basic education. A study done by the Economic Commission for Latin America (CEPAL) established that the business costs of training could be reduced significantly — with a corresponding rise in productivity — as private-sector expenditure in basic education rises. In addition, an educated and trained personnel facilitates the application of eco-efficiency programs, environmental management and clean production within a business.

By and large, it remains clear that improvements to education at all levels are fundamental. Experience has shown that investing in educating and training people, especially women, not only contributes to reducing poverty, but also to maintaining a healthy demographic growth and mitigating negative impacts on the environment. This component of sustainable development should be planned and implemented as a joint policy program between the public and private sectors.

In addition to fostering the collaboration between business and academic institutions, it is necessary to provide leadership as a catalyst for the development of capacities in the private sectors of developing countries, so they can adopt the principles of sustainable development and eco-efficiency. In this respect, it is necessary to promote education and training projects that:

- Improve the level of sustainable development literacy.
- Contribute to the development of local knowledge of the business perspective on eco-efficiency, environmental administration, policy climate for sustainable development, and social responsibility.
- Facilitate partnerships for training and educational activities.
- Facilitate self-sustainable projects for education and training.

The business communities of developing nations should get more involved in the area of sustainable development education, supporting research and sharing with communities the resulting products and ideas. Additionally, the educational lag and its intrinsic relation with an absence of sustainable development could be abated with professional publications, information centers, seminars and the use of information technologies.

Best Regards

Sylvia Pinal

Dr Sylvia Pinal

DEVELOPMENT ALTERNATIVES

The monthly newsletter on issues of sustainable development.

A View from India[42]

Ashok Khosla

It is hard to recall any quarter-century in history during which a comparable revolution in ideas and perceptions has taken place. The relationship between people and nature, heading towards a total breakdown over the past two centuries during which Western, industrial "civilization" has set the model for all to follow, is undergoing a gradual but deep transformation.

In this short period, the conservation community has come a long way. Conservation is now a mainstream concern, the subject of major international conventions and conferences. But conservationists can only have a limited impact until they become much better at handling the inter-relationships among the issues of population, resources, environment and development.

Take, for example, consumption patterns. It is obvious that the goals of conservation clearly cannot be reached with today's urban-industrial lifestyles; nor with the existing disparities of the international economy. Sustainable development implies not only efficient and ecologically sound management of resources, but also the need to establish social equity and political empowerment. What hope is there for this planet if the countries of the South start to consume resources as the North does today? They are not only entitled to do so under any concept of fairness and justice, but are also encouraged to by the forces of the global market. What will be the demographic, social and environmental impact in the longer term if their poverty and marginalization in the global economy further delays the stabilization of their population?

The central goal of our production systems has to be not only the generation of goods and services, but also equally the creation of jobs and the efficient use of natural resources. For the poorer half of this world, this translates into satisfaction of basic needs, generation of income (and purchasing power) and maintaining the productivity of the resource-base.

Today's industrial methods are no good: they involve too much capital. They waste too many resources. They cause too much pollution. And they disrupt too many life-support systems. We need new technology and also a new science of economics. We need to create workplaces, jobs, at one hundredth of the costs of the ones we are creating today in our globalized economy.

In this age of privatization, our economies are beginning to follow the example of the industrialized countries and placing more or less total reliance for development action on the corporate sector. This will leave civil society more and more as a marginal player, useful for creating awareness, participative planning, monitoring and evaluation, but not much else. Unless we quickly develop new and creative niches for ourselves and instruments for generating the income we need to compete in the marketplace of ideas and action, civil society and conservation action will soon go the way of other endangered species over the next decade.   ■

SECTION FOUR

Emerging Themes for Business

Increasingly, business will be required to demonstrate management of environmental and social issues along with traditional financial perfor-mance to secure the social license to operate.

Allan Kupcis, Former President and CEO, Ontario Hydro

IN AN ARTICLE in the *Harvard Business Review*, Stuart Hart of the University of Michigan emphasised that: *'Those who think that sustainability is only a matter of pollution control are missing the bigger picture.'* [43] The roots of the crisis, he argued, were political and social issues that exceeded the mandate and capabilities of any corporation. But the paradox, Hart said, was that *'At the same time, corporations are the only organizations with the resources, the tech-nology, the global reach and, ultimately, the motivation to achieve sustainability.'*

In this section we will therefore review some of these emerging themes on the board agenda.

▶ *Corporate Social Responsibility*

What will give business the social licence to operate in the future? What about governance of multinational corporations with economic power as large as nations? What is the role of busi-ness in respect to the social challenges of the future? What will society demand of business?

▶ *Product Stewardship*

What does this term imply for business, and how widespread is its acceptance? How does it relate to product take-back legislation?

▶ *Sustainable Consumption*

What do consumers really want? How will consumer priorities and preferences change in those 'possible worlds' we described in the scenario exercise? Is the term 'sustainable con-sumption' a contradiction in itself?

▶ *Trade and Environment*

Does global trade encourage or undermine sustainability? Is trade and environment compatible?

▶ *Technology Co-operation*

How important is the technology flow? And what is the role of governments in the move from technology transfer to co-operation?

▶ *Risk and Uncertainty*

Much has been said about the precautionary principle — what does that mean in reality? How should industry handle uncertainty?

These themes raise many questions, not only in board meetings, but at all levels of the corporation.

Carlo Novoponte
Chairman

To: Board Members
From: Carlo Novoponte
Date: March 22, 2000
Subject:

Beyond greening SDX

At our last board meeting, our strategy discussions focused on the emerging trends SDX has to understand and cope with. I was asked after the meeting what I meant by a **"socially responsible company"**. I think such a company must be built on the new concept of eco-efficiency, with its emphasis on doing more with less, but in addition it must have the following characteristics:

- ❐ It is profitable and continues to add environmental and financial value for its shareholders, and it creates wealth in society.

- ❐ It devises management systems which help it measure, monitor and continually improve its performance in contributing to the sustainable development goal.

- ❐ It conforms to best practice in its sector and reports regularly on its social and environmental performance.

- ❐ It has an open and transparent relationship with everyone outside as well as inside the company.

- ❐ It ensures that its decisions are fair and just to those affected, and it encourages full participation and carries out wide consultation with its stakeholders before it acts.

I have asked Peter to outline what items I feel should be on our Agenda as we now enter the new century. I enclose his memo and a number of other papers, provided by Laura Benotti at Government Relations, which I would like to discuss at our strategy retreat.

I look forward to seeing you all next month at our retreat weekend in the Yosemite National Park. Don't forget to bring your hiking boots!

C.J. Novoponte

For attention of:
SDX Board Members

Briefing notes for Strategy
Retreat, 1–2 April, 2000

Peter Kennedy
Chief Executive Officer

To:	Carlo Novoponte <cjn>
From:	Peter Kennedy <ptk>
Date:	March 17, 2000
Subject:	**Corporate Social Responsibility**

Corporate social responsibility is about minimizing the company's adverse impact on the social and physical environment. Corporations have since the early '90s increasingly begun to address this "social license to operate", and the issue of "governance" has increasingly been on board agendas.

The attention the issue has been receiving stems in part from a growing feeling that international, national and local systems of government are increasingly out of step with emerging challenges. In part, too, it reflects some people's concern that capitalism in general, and transnational corporations in particular, are, in some sense, "beyond control."

Governance, in the simplest terms, means government, control or authority, and especially the manner or system of governing. One could extend it to mean the management of an activity by some means, such that a range of desired outcomes is attained.

Certainly governance is not simply the province of state intervention. Instead, it is a function that is performed by a wide variety of public and private, state and non-state, national and international institutions and practices.[44] In the corporate world, governance has lately been much concerned with matters such as the role of independent directors on the board, auditing directors' performance, and relating top executives' pay to the value they help create. But increasingly it is also coming to embrace a company's wider responsibilities to the society of which it is a part.[45]

In a world where some corporations are richer and in some ways more powerful than some sovereign states, the challenge for governance systems is "to give power to those best able to use it" - and to remove it from those who use it poorly or evilly.[46]

A recent joint report issued by the Prince of Wales Business Leaders Forum, the World Bank and UNDP suggested that:

> *Issues of accountability, responsibility and influence lie at the core of the debate on the relationship between the public and private sector, and the linkages between national governance and corporate governance.*
> *It is not government's duty to double-guess individual commercial decisions - but to ensure as best it can that the structure it creates for companies contains checks and balances that are effective in resolving the tensions between differing legitimate claims.*

SustainAbility ©

Defining the triple bottom line of sustainable development

Telephone	Fax	E-mail
+44 171 937 9996	+44 171 937 7447	elkington@
		sustainability.co.uk

Fax Message

To: Joe Miller, Director of Communications, SDX Corporation

Fax: 1-617 000 1452

Date: March 17, 2000

No. of pages 2

Re: **Corporate Leadership and Governance**

Dear Joe,

It was good to see you again at the press briefing last week. A useful session, but it seemed to me that your CEO and some of the more influential NGOs were talking past each other on the issue of governance. Yet you all recognise that this is an area of crucial – and growing – importance.

As you know, the central problem is that – despite the existence of the UN and its many agencies – there is no overall body with the legitimacy and authority to ensure that sustainable development happens around the world. Over the next 10–15 years this gap simply has to be filled. SDX Corporation could become a useful business champion for this process.

That said, the resistance of some national governments – including a couple that have a major impact on your business – to attempts to develop more federal regional structures, as in the case of the EU, suggests that we will be hard-pushed to achieve a sensible form of global governance within the next two decades. In some ways, as ever, it may need to be driven by disaster or some other form of intensely felt need.

In the meantime, as we agreed, business in general – and SDX in particular – must work with all the relevant international government partners, among them the UN, OECD, WTO and the World Bank. The focus must be on ensuring that appropriate standards, systems and – perhaps most importantly – controls are in place as soon as is reasonably practicable.

At the *national* and *local* levels, as we have seen in several countries where you operate, there are growing demands for governance that satisfies some basic minimum standards. We need to work out what the role of an SDX is in this area, too. It seems likely that the frustration with the weakness of global governance systems will spur rising expectations – and challenges – at the regional, national and local levels.

Almost all countries want companies operating within their borders to flourish and grow – to help provide employment, wealth and the consumer goods needed for the 'good life'. To achieve this goal, some governments really are going to have to pull up their socks, both in terms of national and corporate forms of governance. Some years back I was struck by what Jonathan Charkham said in his book *Keeping Good Company*:[47]

> *These aspirations cannot be met unless those firms are competitive internationally in a sustained way, and it is this medium- and long-term perspective that makes good corporate governance so vital. Some would argue that many of those running corporations are not so much the current versions of yesterday's pirates as the heirs of those who built great cathedrals and other similar creations and enterprises that have lasted down the centuries.*

But the triple bottom-line of the sustainability agenda (in terms of financial, environmental and social value added) means that successful boards must test their priorities and performance continuously to see whether they *do* run together.[48] The challenge for national governments and international government agencies will be to evolve intermeshing global, national and corporate governance that help, rather than hinder, them in this task.[49]

My feeling is that these issues should be addressed by the SDX board at one of its meetings later in the year. I would suggest that a couple of the non-executive directors be primed in advance and we might even get a couple of leading NGOs to put their heads together on this and present their case in a kick-off session.

I hope to discuss this with you over the next couple of weeks.

With best wishes,

John Elkington
Chairman

Product Stewardship

SDX INTRANET E-MAIL

Subject: Product Stewardship
Date: Fri, 3 March 2000 11:23:29
From: lbenotti@sdx.web
To: jbower@sdx.web

Laura,

We discussed how product stewardship has moved the responsibility frontier beyond the factory gate. You asked me what this term really meant, and what it has meant for SDX.

The concept originated from Dow Chemical in the early 1970s. Since then, many multinational companies have launched "product stewardship" or "product responsibility" programs, including Hewlett-Packard, Intel Corporation, Xerox Corporation and Northern Telecom.[50]

Product stewardship focuses on "...making environmental, health and safety concerns a priority in all phases of a product's life-cycle, and, as a result, lessening the adverse impact of products on human health and the environment."[51] As outlined in the product responsibility guidelines of companies such as Dow, SC Johnson and 3M, product responsibility begins with research and development, i.e. at the point of a product's conception, and extends through product design, manufacture, marketing, distribution, use, recycling and disposal.

Voluntary product stewardship concepts can become a significant factor in the mindset of all of industry if the policy framework is set right. If not, the pioneers in accepting a widened product responsibility may not gain the competitive advantage that an extended view of the product cycle should yield, seen from a global societal viewpoint.

While product stewardship emphasizes voluntary action, governments can choose to set a complementary framework through the concept of EXTENDED PRODUCT RESPONSIBILITY. EPR aims also at resource conservation and pollution prevention, and - similar to the voluntary stewardship model- also advocates a life-cycle perspective to identify strategic pollution prevention and resource conservation opportunities. The principle of shared responsibility ensures that designers, suppliers, manufacturers, distributors, users and disposers each take responsibility for the environmental impact of products throughout the entire product life.

While product stewardship is voluntary, and thus may not cover all industrial producers (the "free-riders" problem), it is driven by competitive objectives, not only "compliance at least cost." It should, therefore, be more efficient in societal terms. Even if it mainly covers the larger and more visible players, their efforts may be more important as a "demonstration" process with peer-pressure effect. This view is taken by the U.S. President's Council for Sustainable Development: "The greater responsibility rests with the actors who have the greatest ability to influence the environmental and energy impacts of the specific production system, depending upon the product's specific characteristics."[52]

As mentioned above, the life-cycle approach leads to a renewed importance of product stewardship. As the understanding of material flows and energy flows begins to enter the mainstream of daily management, new questions arise: "What happened before?", i.e. where did the raw material come from, and how was it produced, packaged and transported to the business? The same questions are asked at the next link in the resource chain, so the management will be asked to take a moral, if not legal responsibility for goods and services after they leave the factory door.

PRODUCT TAKE-BACK LEGISLATION

You asked me how we see the trends in product take-back. This policy, which requires manufacturers to recover and recycle a wide range of products such as packaging, automobiles, batteries and electronic equipment, is now being developed and applied in Europe, the U.S. and Japan.

Many manufacturers now assume that product take-back will form an inevitable part of business in the future.

Product take-back strategies fit within broader policy frameworks aimed at "closing the materials loop," which is one of SDX's stated long-term goals.

The principal aim of the Japanese "Law for the Promotion of the Re-utilization of Recycled Resources" and the proposed German "Closed-Loop Economy and Waste Management Act" is to increase the overall efficiency of the industrial production and consumption system. This would occur through increasing the use of industrial by-products as feedstocks for other processes, thereby minimizing waste generation and the consumption of raw materials by the system as a whole.

The model for product take-back was first established by the German Packaging Ordinance of 1991. That legislation, as well as similar requirements for electronics and automobiles, placed new obligations on the product chain (retailers, distributors and manufacturers) to take back used products and dispose of them, with preference to re-use and recycling.

As an alternative, the legislation gave industry the option of establishing and financing a collection and recycling system. This is precisely the route German industry took, creating the Duales System Deutschland (DSD), also known as the "Green Dot" program.

WHY IS THIS IMPORTANT FOR SDX?

SDX had already introduced its product stewardship plan in the early '90s, and it has accelerated the pace of change in product design and in the development of "Design for Environment" programs. We, like most companies, are not embarking upon these initiatives purely to meet regulatory requirements. Rather, through design change, we can reduce the cost of complying with these new obligations.

Participation in the German DSD system requires the payment of licensing fees based on the weight of the package and the recyclability of the packaging material. This provides an incentive to evaluate the weight and recyclability of paper and plastic packaging alternatives, among other factors, and may result in a switch from one to the other to reduce costs. A similar analysis would suggest that the cost of recycling an automobile or a computer would be lower if the product took less time to disassemble and contained recyclable material.

Is it relevant for our U.S. operations? I think so because:

• While eco-labeling and producer-responsibility developments have mostly occurred at the national level in Western Europe and Japan, they affect corporate practices and the introduction of "greener" products worldwide. A U.S.-based company must comply with product recycling requirements in Germany or the Netherlands if it is to sell in those markets. The company will also want to apply for a European Union eco-label so that it can compete successfully within the European market.

• The environmental benefits of improved product designs will not be limited to those countries with stricter regulatory regimes because companies often develop products that enter multiple markets.

• As long as a new product design does not cost more or have a negative effect on consumers' perception of the product, such as increased customer satisfaction or reduced production costs, it will probably be sold in other markets as well as in the one it was tailored for.

• In addition, as companies develop further knowledge of "green" design, their experience will be incorporated into principles and tools that are applicable for use company-wide, transcending national boundaries.

I hope the above helps put product take-back and redesign in context.

L.P. Benotti

BRIEFING NOTE

Date: **03-03-2000**

Re: **Extended Producer Responsibility and the Use of Market Forces**

The OECD has highlighted the role of liabilities in avoiding environmental damage. They point out that liability for environmental damage is fundamental to the "polluter pays principle" and that the liability for the management of materials can be established in law through the concept of *extended producer responsibility*. Experiences in the Netherlands have shown that legislation establishing the extended producer responsibility principle can be effective in bringing about technological and organizational innovations. Similarly, German legislation requiring manufacturers to take back durable goods at the end of their life has led to companies moving towards asset recovery, remanufacturing and redesigning.

The use of market forces and economic instruments has led to more focus on incentive-based approaches giving rewards for good performance rather than only punishing poor performance. Some of these measures are fiscal; others use non-fiscal tradable permits or deposit refund schemes, etc. Sweden now taxes batteries, Belgium disposal razors, Italy polythene in carrier bags. Several Scandinavian countries now tax emissions of carbon dioxide, the main greenhouse gas. In Norway, a CO_2 tax is estimated to have reduced emissions of CO_2 from stationary sources by up to 21%. In Denmark, a tax on non-hazardous waste has doubled the cost of waste dumping and incineration.

The trend is increasingly for government to set the goals and standards through negotiation and then to allow flexibility in how to achieve them. The former should not be seen as a means of raising revenue and swelling government coffers, though: revenues raised need to be reinvested in the environment; taxes on the "bads" (i.e. inefficient resource use) need to be compensated by reducing some of the taxes currently falling on the "goods" (i.e. employment).

Historically, it has been easy for companies to dismiss environmental and social costs to the account of society and outside the price of the goods and services provided as an inevitable cost of doing business: as "externalities." Government has a responsibility to ensure that these *costs are internalized* and resource exploitation is reflected in a truer price of goods and services.

inter-office memorandum

To: Jim Peters, Director of Public Affairs <jrp>

From: Laura Benotti, Manager, Government Relations <lpb>

Date: March 10, 2000

Subject:

Consumer wants, marketing and eco-labeling

At last week's government/business/NGO Roundtable we debated recent trends in changing consumption and production patterns. We all agreed that the key to securing a real change towards sustainable development lies in *shifting consumer behavior.*

Through *marketing and advertising* we reach out to the customers and inform them. Many sectors of industry have become very expert in using marketing techniques successfully, but the fact remains that we cannot sell what the consumer does not want. *Market signals* are thus the most effective drivers for changing production patterns and industry's competitive position.

Within this broad market signals category, *eco-labeling* has emerged as one important channel of communication between the producers and consumers. Especially widespread in Europe, Canada and Japan, eco-labeling schemes award "seals of approval" for products which are less harmful to the environment than other products in their class. These programs cover diverse products, ranging from paper products and paints to household appliances and construction materials.

The first eco-label program, the German "Blue Angel," began in 1978. By 1990, the Blue Angel label had been awarded to 3,200 products in 60 product categories and the symbol was recognized by almost 80% of German households.[53]

In response to the proliferation of eco-labeling schemes, the European Union adopted an eco-labeling regulation in 1992 to provide some consistency among member states. The EU eco-label scheme aims to:

- Promote the design, production, marketing and use of products that have a reduced environmental impact during their entire life-cycle.
- Provide consumers with better information on the environmental impact of products.

The program awards eco-labels to products that meet specified environmental performance criteria defined for individual product groups. The criteria are based on an assessment of the product's major environmental impacts *throughout its life-cycle.* For example, the criteria for dishwashers set numerical limits on energy and water consumption, established requirements for marking plastics by polymeric material, and established minimum wash and dry efficiencies.

What is eco-labeling's effect on our business?

Participation in the EU and other eco-labeling programs is voluntary. It is up to each company to complete applications with supporting documentation of the environmental impact for each product that it would like considered for the label.

- This means that obtaining eco-labels can be a costly and time-consuming process, particularly for companies like ours which have to seek eco-labels for multiple national programs with different qualifying requirements.
- Eco-labels require that the consumer understand what the label implies, and that there is an open dialogue between the experts designing criteria for the labels and the manufacturer, who, of course, knows the product best.
- We would all benefit if labels in different countries were standardized to avoid accusations of their being used as so-called "green trade barriers."

To sum up: eco-labels are not a perfect tool for communicating with consumers, but we in SDX have to understand them in order to be competitive on the international market.

I hope that clarifies some of the issues we discussed last week.

Laura Benotti

L.P. Benotti

Sustainable Consumption

Subject: Changes in Consumer Behavior
Date: Mon, 20 March 2000 14:42:05
From: jpeters@sdx.web
To: lbenotti@sdx.web

Laura,

Your note of March 10 triggered a useful debate in my team. Here is a summary of how we see what is happening on that subject right now.

Recession, coupled with controversy about product environmental claims, have buffeted the green consumer movement. Nonetheless, a report to Dow Chemical by SustainAbility suggests that the environmental focus is shifting. It says that:

• In the 1970s, the focus was on "doomsday scenarios" and the assessment of large-scale projects.
• This shifted in the 1980s to plants and processes.
• This production orientation has been joined in the 1990s by an emphasis on products and their life-cycles.
• The next focus, SustainAbility predicts, will be on sustainable consumption and lifestyle patterns as part of a broader move to sustainable economies.[54]

Policy responses

The 1992 Earth Summit in Rio coined a new term, "sustainable consumption," and allied it to production. At first sight this whole concept may seem like a contradiction in terms. However, the following extract may help explain:

...the major cause of the continued deterioration of the global environment is the unsustainable pattern of consumption and production, particularly in industrialized countries.

Achieving the goals of sustainable development will require efficiencies in production and changes in consumption patterns in order to emphasize optimization of resource use and minimization of wastes.

Agenda 21, Chapter 4, of the Rio Earth Summit

Since Rio, governments and non-governmental and business organizations have been trying to unravel the complexities of the consumption and production issue as part of the broader agenda.

• Terms such as "ecological footprints" are suggested by environmental NGOs to define sustainable consumption on a per-capita basis for specific resources.
• The "Sustainable Europe" project calculates "environmental space" as the total global resources that we can use without threatening future generations, allocated equitably among the world's population.
• Von Weizsäcker, Lovins and Lovins proposed that current best available approaches and technologies applied universally could lead to an aggregate Factor Four improvement over today's resource productivities.[55] The "Factor 10 Club" have further suggested that the richest countries need to find ways to improve their resource productivity by at least Factor 10 up to 2050.[56]

Sounds like Star Trek!

Various governments (such as that in the Netherlands) are now considering these elements. But a great deal more work needs to be done if governments are to change regulatory and market policies in an attempt to drive towards sustainable consumption.

How does this affect SDX?

Business will continue to be challenged to meet customer demands while promoting environmental quality. But the consumer will make increasing demands on business. These will extend beyond environmental aspects and will include a critical view on social corporate responsibility.

• Through advertising and marketing, business helps to set trends that influence consumer demand. Also, business itself is a major consumer of natural resources and energy, as well as of goods and services.
• Moving towards more sustainable production and consumption (SP&C for short) will require changes to business operations and decisions, because it is business that ultimately determines the design, manufacture and delivery of goods and services.

Although business has demonstrated its support for SP&C through a variety of voluntary initiatives and programs - as shown by the ICC's broadly supported Business Charter for Sustainable Development - government and NGOs have until now largely shaped the debate.

Ultimately, any initiatives on SP&C will affect business, the provider of goods and services. We in business need to publicize our progress in order to help guide the public agenda so that it does not stifle competition, economic growth and technological innovation.

Thanks again, Laura, for kick-starting our thinking on this complicated subject.

Jim Peters

> **Note:** See Section Six for more on Factor 4 and Factor 10 . . .

ISSN 1999–0000

Vol. 25 Issue 6

INTERNATIONAL MARKETING

The magazine for marketing professionals

6 March 2000

The new consumer question:
Do I need it?

Does consuming "sustainably" mean consuming less, or more? Annoula Louisidou investigates.

More and more companies are nowadays beginning to ask themselves questions such as: "Do our customers really need the *product* the way we have designed it, or do they need another *service*?"

Some postulate that society simply has to learn to consume less. Others point out that if the "less in quantity" is produced, used and disposed of irresponsibly, the net effect could be far worse than a "more" that incorporated eco-efficient practices.

Add to that argument the fact that the growing aspirations of the developing world mean they will ask for more products and you have a major conundrum to resolve.

While there may be a growing market for products, their nature and the means used to advertise and distribute them will be very different from what they are today.

According to many expert observers, there will be a shift from products to services.[57] We see this already in many examples: Xerox switched from selling photocopiers to leasing them, thereby focusing on the performance of the service. Volkswagen has launched a car share option, whereby the owner of a large apartment building is buying several cars (ranging from small electric to large minivan) that are then shared by all in the apartment building. Another example is Interface, a U.S. carpet producer that rents rather than sells carpets, thereby taking over the full responsibility for the performance of the product.

This shows that companies are now adapting their marketing strategies away from a focus on the ownership of products towards the provision of services.

Says Peter Kennedy, CEO of SDX Corporation: "A product should be regarded as what it really is – a means to an end, that of providing value to the customer. The customer's loyalty is not to individual products but to the need for a service.

"The American railroad companies declined because they defined their business around a product, the railway, and not about moving people quickly and comfortably.

"As a result, people abandoned the railway for roads and cars when these could provide that mobility more successfully."

Today, successful businesses are built around the service-content principle. For marketing managers, the challenge is to incorporate environmental considerations into the increasingly complex mix.

Trade and the Environment

inter-office memorandum

To: Laura P. Benotti, Head, Government Relations <lpb>

From: Chuck Domanski, Economics Unit, Corporate Planning <cjd>

Date: March 3, 2000

Subject: Trade and the Environment

You asked for a briefing on this subject in preparation for the meeting you and Mr Kennedy are having next week with the WTO Trade Delegation.

Issues and trends

Trade and environment issues arise when global trade rules intersect with environmental goals and regulations. Two points need to be made right away:

- Freer, more liberal global trade means growth. But in pursuing trade liberalization and growth opportunities we cannot ignore environmental - or social - issues.
- Trade law and environmental law are becoming increasingly interwoven and inseparable.

Recent years have seen a number of international trade disputes triggered by attempts in particular countries to ban certain types of production or to introduce new labeling schemes or restrict certain materials on environmental grounds. As efforts to protect the environment grow, and as the process of globalization continues, the number of such potential conflicts can only increase.

In its report, *Trade and Environment: A Business Perspective*,[58] the WBCSD argues for the establishment of a **bridging mechanism** to harmonize international trade law with multilateral environmental agreements. The report makes the point that acceleration of the process of globalization can only intensify the sensitivity of such issues. For business, one aim is therefore to ensure a level international "playing field" for products and services.

This will facilitate world trade, which will in turn strengthen national economies and make more resources available to tackle environmental and social concerns. In some cases, this harmonization may mean that local or national environmental standards will have to be adjusted, up or down.

Policy responses

A number of industry sectors have formulated *voluntary codes of conduct*. Among them are the chemical industry's Code of Ethics on the International Trade of Chemicals, and the banking industry's Statement by Banks on the Environment and Sustainable Development.

But there are also a growing number of regulations in this field. Indeed, direct restraints on international trade have featured in agreements such as:

- **CITES** (Convention on the International Trade in Endangered Species of Wild Flora and Fauna), which limits the animal and plant species, and their parts, that may be traded internationally.
- The **Montreal Protocol**, which requires parties to phase out the trade in chlorofluorocarbons (CFCs) and other ozone-depleting substances.
- The **Basel Convention** on the Control of Transboundary Movements of Hazardous Wastes and their Disposal. This limits trade directly by restricting the transboundary movement of certain materials, and it includes a ban on the export of recyclable hazardous wastes from OECD to non-OECD countries. Significant debate continues on the meaning of "hazardous" in this context.
- The **International Tropical Timber Agreement**. So far, this is the first and only commodity trade agreement to contain environmental conservation goals, but it will presumably not be the last.

The **World Trade Organization** (WTO) is now responsible for bringing some order into the complicated interrelationship between trade and environmental legislation. **GATT**, the General Agreement on Tariffs and Trade, explicitly recognizes the right of states to protect their own environment from the effects of emissions occurring within their own boundaries - for example, by allowing them to prohibit the import of certain harmful substances. These rights must be exercised specifically, however, and cannot be applied in a discriminatory fashion.

For regulators and campaigners, some of whom are against the process of globalization itself, the issue often comes down to national sovereignty. Surely, they ask, shouldn't countries have the right to set higher environmental standards if they choose to do so? With right often on both sides, these controversies are guaranteed to be a recurrent feature of 21st-century business.

I hope the above helps, but please do call me if there's anything you would like me to elaborate on further.

Chuck Domanski

C.J. Domanski

P.S. I attach a copy of an article from *International Business Issues* which is relevant here.

International Business Issues

A monthly newsletter for business people

FEBRUARY 2000

Trade and environment debate: Why it's important for business

Margaret Flaherty answers some of the questions you may have about trade and sustainable development.

I can see that trade and environmental laws and regulations may affect the way large multinationals do business. But I run a small-scale electronics business in Mexico with aspirations to expand into the rest of the Americas. What do they mean for me?

Whenever global trade increases, new environmental concerns and priorities emerge, and new environmental laws are not far behind. Mexico is no less immune from them than any other country.

For example, environmental taxes, eco-labeling requirements and laws governing areas such as packaging and the recycled-material content of goods clearly affect the way your company must operate, especially if you hope to export to highly developed markets such as the U.S.A.

I've heard it said that concern for the environment poses one of the most significant challenges to trade liberalization and access to foreign markets. Why is this?

Environmental groups are deeply involved in trade issues. Their concerns have become an important factor in drafting European Union law and the North American Free Trade Agreement, and they are at the top of the agenda of the World Trade Organization.

Furthermore, international consumer boycotts have become an effective tool in the hands of environmental groups.

These groups often see the placing of restrictions on trade as a key to both preserving and expanding existing environmental laws and to protecting the environment.

Why are trade and environmental laws colliding and what effect does this have on efforts to liberalize trade?

Laws that promote global trade can be a critical element in a company's growth equation. But as concern about the health of the environment multiplies around the world, trade law is increasingly colliding with environmental law.

Many international environmental agreements are incorporating trade rules which some experts believe conflict with existing trade law. However, for political reasons, governments are often not prepared to challenge these agreements.

At the same time, however, several trade-law cases in the past ten years have challenged domestic environmental laws. The end result of this "collision of laws" is a threat to the continuing liberalization of trade.

Can you give an example of a collision between trade and environmental law?

Eco-labeling programs are the latest example. These programs can restrict or prevent a foreign product from entering a new market *even if it is more environmentally sound than a domestic product if seen in a total life-cycle perspective.* The recycled content requirement is a case in point.

inter-office memorandum

To: Laura Benotti, Manager, Government Relations <lpb>

From: Johannes Bauer, Corporate Legal Dept <jwb>

Date: February 10, 2000

Subject: **Critical future trade and environmental issues**

Recently we hear more and more about conflict, collision and threats to competition due to trade and environment interaction. This interaction focuses on two areas of concern: **market access** and **competitiveness**.

> *Market access* raises the question: Can Country A pass an environmental law that prevents the import of products from Country B based on the way they are grown, manufactured, packaged or disposed of?

> *Competitiveness.* Will a country with low environmental standards lure investment and jobs with the promise that manufacturing costs will be lower due to less stringent standards and enforcement? Will companies operating in countries with high standards suffer a competitive disadvantage in dealing with companies from low-standard countries?

First, some general trends.

1. We are increasingly aware that many types of environmental problems disregard national borders and have transboundary or global effects. This means that individual countries, acting alone, can not fix the problem.
2. Hence, the need for global solutions in the form of international environmental agreements, or in trade parlance, multilateral environmental agreements (MEAs).
3. The "teeth" needed to enforce the "bite" (obligations) of these agreements are limited. To date, trade restrictions seem to be one of the few ways to get countries to sign on and enforce obligations.
4. However, using trade restrictions as the enforcement mechanism is troublesome to those committed to free trade. Supporters of free trade (generally, the business community) fear that hard-won efforts to open markets and keep the flow of goods as unhindered as possible may be lost if new "environmental barriers" are erected.

Although a range of disputes have emerged that illustrate the intersection of trade and environment, one event, the "Tuna–Dolphin" case, triggered a "rallying cry" for the environmental community. The United States banned tunafish because Mexican fishermen caught the fish in a way that accidentally killed large numbers of dolphins. Mexico brought a challenge before the General Agreement on Tariffs and Trade (GATT). The dispute panel ruled that the U.S. was wrong and had violated their trade obligations. For environmentalists, this case provided the "smoking gun": where trade and environment clash, trade will reign supreme and gains on environmental protection will wither and die.[59]

Environmental perspective vs free trade perspective

Trade liberalization and environmental protection policies are already quite complex in their own right and have had enormous efforts devoted to furthering their respective aims. When considered within separate policy spheres, these aims have often conflicted, leaving politicians and environmental NGOs at odds; the commercial impact is generally mixed, depending on which side of the border you stand. This problem has been caused in part by the fact that trade regimes have generally derived from international collaboration, while environmental protection policies have largely originated at the domestic level. Domestic environmental policies have almost inevitably led to restrictions on the free flow of trade. However, trade liberalization and environmental protection together are now seen as essential to global "sustainable development."

To illustrate this divide, those advocating a strong environmental perspective say, "Trade means growth and expansion of industrial activity. This will mean more pollution and consumption of non-renewable resources." To which the trade folks say, "Hogwash. Trade provides higher levels of wealth to support environmental activities and open trade enables the flow of technology which, in turn, encourages new environmentally beneficial technologies." The voices of pro-trade claim, "Environmental regulations will be used as a façade to conceal discriminatory or protectionist trade agendas – environmental regulations will become a guise for trade protectionism and, given how hard it is to keep markets open, the prospect of giving the protectionist a new set of excuses is worrisome." Environmentalists counter, "Environmental regulations, including international agreements that contain trade sanctions, are necessary to enforce international environmental agreements and to reinforce environmental policies." And so on.

Another factor that contributes to clashes on trade and environment is the fact that it involves two very different policy disciplines and theoretical foundations. The GATT, now World Trade Organization, was secretive, diplomatic and economics-oriented. The environmental traditions are more law-oriented with a strong belief in public participation and transparency in the policy process, with policies often derived from a sense of moral obligation.

Notwithstanding the apparent gulf between the proponents of free trade and environmental protection, those on either side of the debate must sooner or later come to accept the following assertions:

1. Environmental protection is vital to preserving the planet as we know it, and for maintaining quality of human life over successive generations.
2. Free and liberalized trade between the different nations of the world is equally as important to the economic well-being of all nations, as well as for quality of life.
3. Neither of the foregoing is indefinitely sustainable without the other.

And while most reasonable people may accept these statements, many in business and industry fear that environmental regulation will be used not for the furtherance of the important and worthy goal of sustained human preservation, but rather as the "Trojan Horse" of protectionism. In fact, many countries have become extraordinarily interested in the production and process methods of goods produced far from their shores, as much as a result of their appreciation that pollution does not recognize national borders (often leaving polluters beyond the regulatory enforcement powers of those who suffer the pollution) than as a way to disguise their protectionist schemes. But the GATT does not allow individual parties to sanction other parties for pollution caused outside their own borders.

At the same time, many environmentalists suspect that all business is interested in is bottom-line profits, no matter what the ultimate cost to the continuation of the planet in liveable form.

While the truth of both of the above assertions is infinitely disputable, what isn't is the reality that economic development, bolstered and spread by liberalized trade, and sound environmental management techniques are complimentary aspects of the same agenda. The case examples contained herein will attempt to illustrate this concept, as well as the impact of the trade and environment debate on the finance and banking sector.

How would a conflict arise?

There are two mechanisms that may give rise to a trade and environment conflict. The first is through a global agreement developed to address an environmental concern, such as the Basel Convention (designed to eliminate the environmental risks arising from the transboundary movement of hazardous waste), the Montreal Protocol (designed to protect the ozone layer from continued deterioration caused by man-made chemical emissions) or the Biodiversity Convention (designed to encourage the sustainable use of biological diversity).

These types of MEAs are enforced through the imposition of trade-restrictive measures against the offending nation. Since most of the conduct punishable under the various MEAs occurs outside the borders of the country wishing to sanction the polluting country, the sanctions specifically authorized under the MEAs would appear to be in direct contravention with the GATT. Further complicating matters is the fact that most of the signatories to the GATT are also signatories to most if not all of the MEAs. Although no case has yet been decided by the GATT dispute panel where a trade measure imposed pursuant to an MEA is alleged to be violative of the GATT, the majority opinion is that such a panel would hold the MEA trade measure illegal.

The second mechanism giving rise to conflict occurs when a country acts alone, or unilaterally, and passes a law with the ostensible purpose of protecting that country's own environment. Such measures, also often enforced through trade restrictions, are allowed under GATT so long as the host country holds goods produced within its own borders to the same standards. However, a unilateral measure will not pass muster under GATT if their primary purpose and/or result is the protection of domestic markets.

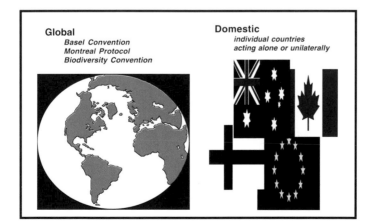

Some nuts and bolts of the GATT

The General Agreement on Tariffs and Trade (GATT) has been employed over the last 48 years as the pre-eminent liberalizer of world trade. But the GATT is not an international organization like the UN or the World Intellectual Property Organization, nor does it have any members, nor does it have the legal status of a treaty or charter. Rather, it is merely a multilateral agreement between contracting governments.

Since the GATT's inception, eight separate rounds of trade liberalization talks have been held between the parties, with each resulting in a further lowering of innumerable trade barriers or tariffs. The most recent one was the "Uruguay Round," concluded after seven years of haggling. Despite its loose structure, the GATT has been a success in assisting the increase in world trade. Between 1965 and 1990, worldwide exports grew by 439%, and overall world production by 136%.

The negotiators agreed upon the creation of the WTO, codifying the legal structure of the GATT secretariat which had always had a mere *ad hoc* existence. The WTO does not have the authority to usurp national sovereign power on matters of trade. Modifications to GATT must still be made by consensus of all the contracting governments, and in the event of a contracting party refusing to accept the judgement of a GATT dispute panel, the WTO has no legal authority or police power to enforce such decision, except through its coercive ability to allow other contracting powers to legally impose (under GATT) economic sanctions (in the form of higher trade barriers) against the non-compliant offender.

The "pillars" of the GATT

How does the GATT function? It is designed solely to redress trade restrictions and distortions; it has no effect on the content of traded goods, and its agreements apply to any kind of product. It is also an agreement between governments and not private companies or trade associations.

The three most important principles of the GATT are:

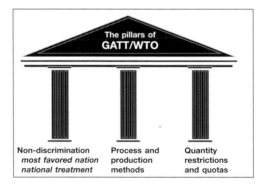

Non-discrimination
There are two principles of non-discrimination: most favored nation and national treatment. Taken together, they require products from one foreign country to be treated in the same way as products from any other foreign country, and in turn in the same way as those

manufactured in the importing country. For example, France must hold beer imported from Germany to the same standard as it would hold beer imported from Spain and similarly, it must apply the same standard to its own French-made beer. The intention is to eliminate favoritism between all GATT parties.

Product vs process methods

A trade restriction distinction *cannot* be based on the method used to process or produce the traded goods; it must relate directly to such goods. (For example, the noted "Tuna–Dolphin GATT Panel" cases revolved around the U.S.'s attempt to prohibit the import of Mexican tuna because of the way the fish were caught [with drift nets which also caused a large number of dolphin deaths]. Mexico successfully claimed that the trade restriction was illegal because it was based on the method in which the goods were produced, as opposed to a defect inherent in the tuna. Had the U.S. prohibited the import of Mexican tuna claiming it contained elevated mercury levels, the ban would have passed GATT muster.)

Prohibition on quantitative measures and restrictions

Simply put, the GATT prohibits the use of trade-limiting embargoes and/or quotas between contracting parties.

Market size is muscle

As one may expect, the above components of GATT are not absolute. A contracting party may ignore them if the measure is necessary to the protection of the life or health of humans, plants or animals. Such measures may also be taken if they are reasonably related to conserving exhaustible natural resources, so long as such restrictions are applied to the acting party's own use of the resource and only if they are the least restrictive trade measure reasonably available.

Practically speaking, the bigger your economy, the less you have to abide by the rules. The major trading powers have fewer fears of trade measures being used unilaterally against them for environmental purposes. For the small and medium-sized trading countries, this raises concerns both about the equity of allowing unilateral measures to be taken and about the ability of the major powers to use those measures for protectionist or competitiveness reasons unrelated to environmental factors.

Johannes Bauer

Intergovernmental Panel on Industry

1 Industry Plaza, New York, NY 99999   Tel: 999 1119999   Fax: 999 2229999   http://xyz.ipi.web

BRIEFING NOTE

Date: **03-18-2000**

Re: **Trade Liberalization and the Environment**

As a background to the upcoming negotiations, here are some comments on liberalization as seen from our perspective.

Liberalization of international trade accentuates the need for a new government role.
Trade as an instrument of economic growth has the potential to increase financial and technological resources available for development and environmental protection. However, the consequent emphasis on price competitiveness could also push environmental and developmental concerns down the list of national priorities. Unfettered free trade may result in policy or market failures which result in the underpricing and short-term, unsustainable over-exploitation of natural resources for export.

On the other hand, a fear exists that, as national environmental regulations become more stringent, some countries may be unable to compete with others who have lower standards and consequently lower prices. Concern is also expressed that the environment may be used as a new form of token "green protectionism" protecting domestic producers. All of these arguments and the others that surround the issue of trade point to a critical role for government to ensure environmental interests are protected.

It is clear that, in spite of many initiatives to reverse the trend, inequitable distribution of resources will continue well into the future. Sustainable development will only be realized and sustained if equity issues are addressed both inter-generationally and within generations. Conflicts over scarce resources will increase as trends in population growth and resource depletion continue. Conflict resolution through arbitration, mediation and empowering and protecting the rights of the disadvantaged can only be realistically achieved by the nation's principle custodians: government.

The traditional role of government will, of course, still continue: that of command and control – legislating and enforcing legislation. In compliance-driven systems – such as the U.S. – it will assume more importance than it does in other countries.

These countries will need to work out their own formulae and mix between prescriptive legislation and more incentive-based approaches such as economic instruments and voluntary agreements.

In many developing countries, the difficulties of enforcement capacity creates a need for alternatives. This is exacerbated by the recognition that enforcement is tending to be recognized as a responsibility of lower tiers of government. In some countries (as in the case of the Australian mining industry, for example), the standards are set by one ministry (the Ministry of the Environment) but enforced by another (the Ministry of Industry).

However, many multinational companies now profess to be applying the same standards at home as they would overseas. The UN's benchmark survey of multinationals in 1993 found that "...regulations in the home country [are] the single most important factor in the development of corporate side global environmental standards."[60]

In whichever situation, legislation is needed to set absolute minimum standards beyond which penalties will be enforced and severe. In some instances, these minimum standards will be quite high, as in the case of transport of hazardous materials, for example. Many companies now recognize the need to be innovative beyond compliance and governments need to establish the right climate in which this can be successful.

Technology Co-operation

SDX Technology Research Laboratories

Prof. Okito Yamahasi, Chief Scientist

Laura P. Benotti
Government Relations
SDX Corporation
SDX Technology Park
Cambridge, MA 10000

March 4, 2000

Dear Laura,

In response to your recent telephone call, here are my thoughts on technology development and co-operation. I'll be happy to give you more detail if you need it.

As I see it, the sustainable corporation will continuously have to re-invent its technology-base. The concepts of **cleaner production** and **eco-efficiency** are crucial in that process. They are relevant not only to multinational manufacturing and service companies but also to the small and medium-sized enterprises, which are the backbone of economic development in the developing world.

Competitiveness in the 21st century will depend very much on resource efficiency, as outlined by Prof. Michael Porter when he said: "Cleaner production is about investing to create value through foresight, instead of spending money in hindsight to limit and repair the environmental damage."[61]

The diffusion of technology and competence will set the pace and character of future economic growth, especially in developing countries. Whether an environmental dimension can be injected into these efforts will determine if this growth will be sustainable or not.

Technology enables people to create more from less. New technology is usually cleaner than the old because it is designed for efficiency.

But putting the latest technology to work where it is needed most - mainly in the developing world and in economies in transition - is often difficult because of a lack of money, skills and suitable investment frameworks.

Simply giving new technologies to those who need it through aid schemes, as was tried in the 1960s and 1970s, has been shown to be ineffective. Building partnerships between those with the technology and those who need it - through joint ventures and foreign direct investment, for example - is a better way because both parties have an interest in the success of the project.

Many believe that companies in developing countries, which already have a labor cost advantage, could benefit from "leapfrog" technology that develops and adds *cleaner production* to their strategy. *Cleaner production*, as defined and promoted by the United Nations Environment Program (UNEP) is the continuous application of an integrated preventative environmental strategy applied to processes, products and services to increase eco-efficiency and reduce risks for humans and the environment.

Cleaner production applies to:

- **Production processes** - conserving raw materials and energy, eliminating toxic raw materials and reducing waste and toxicity emissions
- **Products** - reducing negative impacts throughout the life-cycle of a product
- **Services**

UNEP has operated its Industry and Environment center (UNEP IE) since 1975 to promote cleaner and safer industrial production and consumption patterns. Its objective is to spread these concepts to industries around the world, especially in developing countries and economies in transition, in order to make those industries more competitive in the future. As a result of its 25 years-plus of work around the globe, UNEP has changed the mental map of many small and large businesses from an "end-of-pipe" compliance attitude.

Technology co-operation between companies was identified by the WBCSD at the 1992 Earth Summit as the critical mechanism for promoting sustainable development. Governments agreed that technology co-operation must concentrate on developing human resources by extending a country's ability to absorb, generate and apply knowledge. In developing countries, it must be designed to help enhance the use of technology, promote innovation and *foster entrepreneurship*.

Past government-to-government technology transfer programs under Foreign Aid schemes have, however, had very limited success. Real co-operation works best through long-term business-to-business partnerships that ensure both parties remain committed to the continued success of the project. But this can only happen if the financial and legal climate encourages the prosperity of those partnerships.

The liberalization of the world trade in goods therefore needs to be supported by a liberalization of capital flows, combined with policy changes that can make emerging economies more supportive of investments, entrepreneurs and trade.

What is the business experience so far?
ABB has been co-operating with Polish energy producers to improve their efficiency and environmental performance. Volkswagen of Germany, through its ownership of Skoda, the Czech car maker, has helped improve quality, reduce environmental impact and save what was an ailing business with outdated products. In the U.S., Harry Pearce, Vice Chairman of General Motors, has said: "Cleaner production techniques and strategies are being transferred to local employees and professionals in Thailand and China via hands-on learning and classroom training. Employees of new ventures learn about pollution prevention and waste elimination. These educational programs are helping to train the current and upcoming industry leaders."

These examples show that there are rapidly expanding business opportunities for those companies that are willing and foresighted enough to share best practice and develop sustainable technology solutions for the global market.

With best regards,
Yours truly,

Okito Yamahasi

International Business Issues

A monthly newsletter for business people

MARCH 2000

Technology co-operation: Business's role

The capital invested directly in projects exceeds the value of foreign aid several times over. Is there a need for government-sponsored technology transfer programs? Rachel Semple investigates.

THE MULTITUDE of government-sponsored technology transfer initiatives show that there is a widely recognized and critical need for technology co-operation for the transition economies and the developing countries.

Yet the global aid budget of governments pales into insignificance alongside other major areas of expenditure, particularly defense and the more mundane areas of consumer expenditure.

In the U.S., for example, residential home-owners spend about $7.5 billion a year – equivalent to three-quarters of the U.S. foreign development aid – on caring for their lawns. Families in the industrialized countries spend about $9 billion a year on video games for their children.[62]

While government aid may have a role to play, private capital investment is already far larger and much more effective, if only because private enterprises continue working after making an investment in order to realize a return.

Why is this important?

Technology transfer is important for business first of all because it can be implemented immediately and practically and yields direct results.

Today, a growing number of small and medium-sized enterprises (SMEs) understand that cleaner production is a tool of international competitiveness, and thus is simply *good management*. Cleaner production can therefore make SMEs, which are often the core suppliers of major corporations, more competitive.

The impact of new communication technologies

The next century will see a new phase of business globalization through the rapid dissemination of technological knowledge via the Internet and satellites, thereby creating a "global village" for technology and knowledge access.

But technology co-operation is not only a North–South affair. There are growing examples to be found within the developing world and even between sectors of business within a single country.

The rising foreign direct investment in Central and Eastern Europe will encourage the setting-up of more and more joint ventures and technology co-operation deals with a sustainable development dimension

Let's look at the implications for SDX

Risk and Uncertainty

stevens associates

W. Ross Stevens III

209 Medford Road
Wilmington, DE 19803

March 10, 2000

Mr P. Kennedy
Chief Executive
SDX Corporation
SDX Technology Park
Cambridge, MA 10000

Dear Peter,

Re: Risk, uncertainty and the precautionary principle

You asked us to prepare a briefing note on risk and uncertainty, a theme that has come more and more into the business arena, especially insofar as it is linked to the climate debate.

Let me start with a slightly academic introduction. Many natural systems, such as the atmosphere and the oceans, are by their very nature chaotic. This makes it very difficult to make any hard-and-fast predictions about them. One needs look no further than the inaccuracies in weather forecasting to see the truth of that assertion. The issue of risk is further compounded by rapidly changing technology.

Risk, defined as the probability of suffering harm from hazards, seems at first sight to be highly objective. The perception of it by people is, however, intensely subjective. People worry about some risks in a way that is out of all proportion to the actual potential for harm; meanwhile, they ignore other much more dangerous risks. For example, what is the benefit of bottled water in comparison to water from municipal supplies in Western countries like ours? How much healthier is it? By what degree does it taste better? To many people it is worth a premium of almost 10,000 in price - probably much greater than the objective benefit or reduction in risk.

Business is, of course, used to dealing with risks and uncertainties. Management science has developed tools for handling both uncertainty and risk. Engineering calculations, marketing strategies, accident and loss prevention, financial hedging, credit management, product liability and so on are all well-honed business techniques that manage the various underlying risks and uncertainties.

Indeed, you might argue that business makes its margin by juggling the risk–reward equation. Risk has to be controlled. Industrial corporations tend to insure themselves against most types of risks such as fire and accidents. Banks hedge against currency risk, and insurance companies spread the risk through pooling and syndication. Uncertainty, on the other hand, is often regarded as the basis of opportunities, such as the exploration of new oil and gas fields, the introduction of a new product, or the deployment of a new marketing strategy.

Business challenges

So, while companies handle risk and uncertainty as part of their daily management process, the public's perception of industrial risk, risk management and emergency preparedness is often unclear. Risks that are "dreaded," uncontrollable or not observable by those exposed to them are most likely to generate calls for government intervention. Many environmental problems possess these attributes.[63]

This makes it important to communicate the risks and the way they are managed clearly to those who believe themselves to be impacted by them — their stakeholders. However, many managers underestimate the complexities of putting in place a company program to manage the public perception of how well the company is tackling the issue. On the other hand, some business sectors have focused early on the need to communicate the risk aspects of their business.

Take, for example, the chemicals industry's *Responsible Care*® program. This comprehensive environmental health and safety improvement initiative is not an add-on program but an obligation of membership for many chemical manufacturers' associations around the world. The initiative is built around ten guiding principles, but also includes a commitment to the fulfillment of codes of management practice in key stewardship areas including process and employee safety, environmental protection, distribution of products and other materials, and stakeholder relations.

The precautionary approach

These are all examples of a natural tendency in business to take a precautionary approach to recognized risks and uncertainties. No business is successful in the long term if it fails to take precautionary measures to hedge major risks and uncertainties, even where the science is incomplete, the market imperfectly understood, or the law still emerging.

Responsible Care is really a precautionary strategy to hedge both collective risk within a global industry, and individual risks within a given company. Product testing, design for process safety, marketing with condition of use requirements are all also generally recognized precautionary approaches that companies take today in defense of traditional safety, environmental or legal risks.

What many scientists and stakeholders are concerned about today through advocacy of the "Precautionary Principle" is that our business calculus should include consideration of non-traditional risks, both to our companies and to society at large. I challenge the SDX Corporation to consider the risk of serious, irreversible harm to the natural climate from greenhouse gas emissions; to the integrity of natural ecosystems through ill-considered development; from materials that persist in the environment after their intended use; from materials that can interfere in subtle ways with living systems even at low concentrations, such as in endocrine systems; or from businesses that depend exclusively on material consumption to generate value.

What are the right precautions to take in the face of these uncertain risks? You may wish to calculate the "weighted" expected value of waiting or of taking action. Or you may want to "hedge" and be on the precautionary side, adopting the philosophy of "better safe than sorry." SDX will have to explore them, and in doing so will discover that each offers at least as many opportunities for business value as it does downside risk. As you explore these risks, I am certain that you will then initiate precautionary actions both within SDX and possibly in a larger framework.

Best regards,

SECTION FIVE

Business Concepts for the 21st Century

> *Businesses grounded in the old model will become obsolete and die. At Monsanto, we're trying to invent some new businesses around the concept of sustainability. We may not yet know exactly what those businesses will look like, but we're willing to place some bets because the world cannot avoid needing sustainability in the long run.*
>
> Robert Shapiro, CEO of Monsanto

TWENTY-FIRST-CENTURY CORPORATIONS will need to manage the 'triple bottom-line' of sustainable business, a phrase coined by John Elkington of SustainAbility Ltd. As well as managing the conventional financial bottom-line, they will have to pay more and more attention to social and environmental bottom-lines. In short, they will need to move simultaneously towards economic prosperity, environmental quality and social equity.

Some of the most challenging issues, however, will surface where the three bottom-lines meet.[64] So, for example, economic–environment issues include eco-efficiency, ecological tax reform and environmental accounting; environmental–social issues include environmental justice and inter-generational equity; and social–economic issues include business ethics, human and minority rights.

What concepts will be guiding the successful companies into the new century? We asked some of the corporations involved in the WBCSD scenario project to describe what would be key factors of success. They believe that *eco-efficiency* will be a dominant business philosophy, and that integrated concepts such as *by-product synergy* will spread. New financial models are needed to create *sustainable shareholder value*. To achieve this they call for *new partnerships* with governments and other stakeholders.

The social licence to operate will be another important element for business in the next century. To achieve this, we need *new partnerships* with governments and other stakeholders.

Those are the issues we want to review in this section.

Peter Kennedy
Chief Executive Officer

Corinne Hamilton
Intracapital Inc.
PO Box 301
Amsterdam, The Netherlands

April 6, 2000

Dear Corinne,

Thank you for the valuable contribution you made at last month's International Advisory Council meeting.

There is much debate about the appropriate responsibilities of governments, business and citizens' groups and it is not clear how this will be resolved. But a growing number of business leaders realize that *"to achieve market success they must honor a changing array of environmental and social responsibilities."*[65]

Economic growth remains a vital part of sustainable development. Essentially, it is needed to ensure that poorer, but expanding, populations can improve their quality of life and satisfy their essential needs. So we need growth. But a key idea is that development does not necessarily imply a greater consumption of resources but that it can increasingly be obtained by boosting the quality and efficiency of goods and services. That's why SDX has been pushing the idea of *eco-efficiency* throughout our group.

More and more companies are now measuring their progress towards some aspects of sustainable development. (You will find more about this in the memo from Piotr Kalinskij on Stakeholder Relations.) But most of these measures relate narrowly to the environmental bottom-line, whereas I think we both agree that sustainable development has a wider compass than that.

We have had some interesting and thought-provoking exchanges of ideas both within our group and with governments and grass-root organizations. I attach copies of some these and should be very interested to hear your views.

Best regards,

(signature)

. . . April 6th, 2000 . . .

Eco-Efficiency

SDX Corporation
SDX Technology Park,
Cambridge MA 10000

Tel: 617-000-1111   Fax: 617-000-1486   http://xyz.sdx.web

FAX MESSAGE

To:	Joseph Strand, Business Journalist, *The International Herald Tribune*
From:	Heinrich Neubauer, VP, Operations
Date:	April 26, 2000
No. of pages:	2
Subject:	Eco-efficiency

Dear Joe,

In yesterday's interview you asked me: Can SDX be run eco-efficiently? My answer was: No -
it *must* be run eco-efficiently! If it isn't, we will lose the competitive advantages we have built
up over the last few years in our environment-oriented strategy.

As you know, eco-efficiency has been adopted as a watchword by several leading companies,
including some of our competitors. So we cannot afford to sit still.

I promised to give you some more background: The term "eco-efficiency" was coined in 1992
by the Business Council for Sustainable Development (now the WBCSD) in its ground-
breaking book, *Changing Course*.[66]

PRODUCING MORE WITH LESS

In simple terms, eco-efficiency is about producing more value with fewer resources and less
waste and pollution. But it goes further than that and encourages businesses to become
more competitive, more innovative and more environmentally responsible.

Its goal is to create value for society and the company by doing more with less over the life-
cycle of a product or a service.

Eco-efficiency is designed to help companies support sustainable development and has
been taken up by many corporations and business schools. It is also one of the defining
principles in two recently launched investment funds.

And, very significantly, the 1992 Earth Summit in Rio de Janeiro endorsed eco-efficiency as
being the most important way for industry to contribute to sustainable development.

THE CHALLENGE TO OUR BUSINESS

The eco-efficiency concept challenges our company in seven areas. It requires us to:

- Reduce the amount of material in our goods and services.
- Reduce the energy used in our goods and services.
- Reduce our dispersion toxic wastes.
- Enhance the recyclability of our products.
- Maximize sustainable use of renewable resources.
- Extend our products' durability.
- Increase the "service intensity" of goods and services.

Eco-efficiency encourages all these actions by allowing our business to adapt to new ways of working without immediately abandoning their traditional practices. Furthermore, the philosophy harnesses the business concept of value creation. And that is why we are in business, isn't it?

Best regards

(signature) Heinrich

PS: I will send you an article that appeared recently in *SDX World*.

From the WBCSD Report on Eco-Efficiency . . .

Eco-efficiency is reached by the delivery of competitively priced goods and services that satisfy human needs and bring quality of life, while progressively reducing ecological impacts and resource intensity throughout the life-cycle, to a level in line with the earth's estimated carrying capacity.

Extract from *SDX World* magazine, March 2000 . . .

ECO-EFFICIENCY

Can SDX be run eco-efficiently?

Heinrich Neubauer, VP Operations, asks whether SDX has what it takes to be an eco-efficient company.

"The principle of eco-efficiency is a prerequisite for survival in markets characterized by fierce international competition," says Fritz Gerber, chairman of Hoffmann–LaRoche. "Products and services must be supplied to the market not only at the lowest possible cost but also with efficient use of raw materials and energy."

Why is this important for SDX?

There are several good reasons for adopting eco-efficiency as a way of life here in SDX.

● **It gives us competitive advantage.**

Looking at your business from an environmental perspective in order to optimize *eco-nomical* and *eco-logical* efficiency can be a most powerful way to ask yourself new, sophisticated and testing questions.

Finding the answer to these questions is the key to using all your input factors in an ever more efficient and productive way.

Samuel Johnson, chairman of S.C. Johnson & Son, makers of Johnson's Wax, puts it this way:

We aggressively seek out eco-efficiencies, ways of doing more with less because it makes us more competitive when we reduce and eliminate waste and risk from our products and processes.

Both in the upstream and downstream direction of SDX's business, an "eco-efficient mindset" can

- Reduce the number of inputs we use
- Significantly simplify our processes
- Reduce exposure
- Speed up time to market
- Cut our costs

● The concept fits the way we work.

Eco-efficiency asks sweeping questions in an iterative fashion – in the same way that the last 40 years of total quality management have taught us to do.

Boundary questions, process improvements, functional use of product or service, improvement assessment – all these concepts apply equally well to continuous quality improvement *and* eco-efficiency.

● It is a tool for learning.

Eco-efficiency is not a normative procedure that measures how close you are to some ideal. It is a *learning tool* to make things visible.

The most valuable result of an "eco-efficiency mindset" is the identification of strategic and operational weak spots in one's business, together with the provision of ideas on how to eliminate them.

According to Livio DeSimone, chairman and CEO of 3M:

Each new product, and its associated production process, will be developed with consideration for the elements of eco-efficiency, reducing impact on the environment and improving use of natural resources while meeting our customers' needs and returning a profit to the corporation.

● Who is at the cutting edge?

A growing number of companies are now competing for leadership in the area of eco-efficiency.

ABB emerged as a early pioneer of eco-efficiency in the area of energy-supply technology. Its corporate environmental reports pay particular attention to eco-efficiency:

"High-efficiency, low-emission electrical technology – eco-efficient technology – is vital to achieving global economic and environmental goals in a sustainable manner," says Göran Lindahl, CEO of ABB.[67]

> ❝ *Eco-efficiency is not just about producing what you always produced, only more efficiently. It is also about producing something completely new for which you see a need.* ❞

For a close-up sense of eco-efficiency in practice, Dow Europe[68] provides a good example. Dow Vice President, Claude Fussler, has published much of the intellectual capital the company has developed in this area in his book *Driving Eco-Innovation.*[69]

A key management tool developed by Dow is the "Eco-Compass," which focuses on six dimensions of a product's performance: health and environmental risk; resource conservation; energy intensity; materials intensity; revalorization (remanufacturing, re-use and recycling); and service extension.

The eco-compass is not for stand-alone use but can be applied when comparing one existing product with another, or when comparing a current product with new development options.

The output is six scores and a "map" of the environmental attributes of both the base-case and the comparison product or service.

● What are the lessons?

Eco-efficiency is not a template to be followed blindly. It is a process of seriously asking fundamental questions.

Eco-efficiency is not just about producing what you always produced, only more efficiently. It is also about producing something completely new for which you see a need.

The similarities to "quality" are striking. Here at SDX we believe quality is not an add-on but that it should be deeply embedded in what we produce and sell. You arrive at a high-quality product or service by relentlessly asking questions about what you do, how, and why.

The answers to those questions lead you to better products, new products, new markets – the process is an innovative filter. In this way, eco-efficiency becomes an innovative driver that leads to competitive advantage.

Another strategic advantage of using eco-efficiency in order to shift from product to service is simplification. Profit is no longer a percentage of sales (the "margin"), it's the *gap* between what customers are willing to pay and the cost of the input factors.

For all these reasons, I think we must make sure that eco-efficiency and the eco-innovation process become part of our everyday lives here in SDX.

We can't afford not to![70]

By-Product Synergy

The Business Council for Sustainable Development—Gulf of Mexico
8303 North MoPac Blvd, Austin TX 78759

Heinrich Neubauer
Vice President, Operations
SDX Corporation
SDX Technology Park
Cambridge MA 10000

Austin, May 12, 2000

Dear Mr Neubauer

I read with interest your article in the latest *SDX World* magazine, and share with you the view that eco-efficiency is really about thinking innovatively.

The objective of sustainable development is to bring environmental quality and economic growth into harmony, not conflict. One approach is "green twinning" or "industrial symbiosis" which the BCSD Gulf of Mexico has formulated as "the synergy among different industries, agriculture and communities resulting in profitable conversion of by-products and wastes to resources promoting sustainability." Or, in short, "by-product synergy."

The most cited example of a pioneering effort in this area is the Kalundborg Industrial Park in Denmark, where a series of businesses formed a complex network of waste and energy exchange (see attached summary).

Through analysing and evaluating a number of case studies, our organization has identified six fundamental principles that are needed to successfully practise by-product synergy: *collaboration*, *motivation*, *communication*, *innovation*, *participation* and *evaluation*.

Whereas traditional pollution prevention activities focus on reduction, re-use and recycling within a process, by-product synergy takes pollution prevention "beyond the fence-line" between different processes.

By-product synergy can occur

- Among different organizations;
- Within an organization, but among different business or operating units; or
- Within a business or operating unit, but among different process units.

How the concept can be applied to actual operations can be illustrated by the examples of two of our members:

... May 12th, 2000 ...

---

*In seeking zero waste/100% steel production, **CHAPARRAL STEEL COMPANY** has significantly increased profits while concentrating on environmental issues. For example, Chaparral is using a process in which one of its by-products, slag, is used as a resource in the manufacture of cement, thereby reducing energy consumption, conserving natural resources, and lowering greenhouse gas emissions.*

---

*The Central Reclamation and Salvage Department of **FLORIDA POWER & LIGHT COMPANY** (FPL) collaborates with regional businesses in converting various by-products and wastes from its operations and maintenance activities to resources for other applications, This operation is now a profit center for FPL.*

One example is the large quantities of porcelain generated from old insulation and electrical equipment with porcelain brushing. In a partnership with Eakins Construction Company, the porcelain is now crushed and sold to road-builders. FPL saves hundreds of thousands of dollars a year in landfill costs.

I am sure the SDX Corporation can gain major cost advantages and reduce the impact on the environment if you apply these thoughts in your new factory plans, which the trade journals rumor about. It's a question of attitude: ***by-product synergy is successful not because of the technology, but because of the psychology.***

With best regards

Andy Mangan,
Executive Director of the BCSD–Gulf of Mexico.

Attachment: an example of by-product synergy

The Kalundborg Eco-Industrial Park

The Asnaes coal-fired electric power plant supplies steam to the Novo Nordisk pharmaceutical plant and the Statoil refinery, and waste heat to a district heating system serving 3,500 homes. The refinery removes sulfur from its natural gas, selling it to Kemira, a sulfuric acid manufacturer, resulting in a cleaner gas that is in turn bought by Asnaes. Asnaes sells fly ash to a cement plant and waste gypsum to a wallboard plant, and uses still more waste heat in the greenhouses and fish farms it operates. Sludge from Novo Nordisk becomes fertilizer for local agriculture, and refinery waste water feeds the power plant.

inter-office memorandum sdx

To: Operations managers

From: Heinrich Neubauer, Vice-President, Operations

Date: June 2, 2000

Subject: Eco-efficiency and by-product synergy

Beginning two weeks from now, I would like to review with each of you the potential applications of the eco-efficiency and by-product synergy concepts in your division.

The operations planning team has compiled two checklists to help you understand what these highly interesting approaches could mean for your division.

CHECKLIST

What makes by-product-synergy a success?

☐ Collaboration

The profitable conversion of by-products and wastes to resources requires creative collaboration among generators and consumers.

By-products and wastes may be converted to resources by partners in one–one, one–many, or many–many relationships. Potential partners in by-product synergy project collaboration may be businesses, community organizations, and government agencies.

☐ Motivation

Because it crosses organizational boundaries and requires a change in the status quo, by-product synergy may be met with negative reactions including scepticism, cynicism and anxiety. For a collaboration to be successful, all project stakeholders at all organizations must be motivated to support it.

Motivating people requires changing the organizational structure from one that resists change to one that embraces it. This change in culture must start at the top with the attitude of the organization's senior leadership.

☐ Communication

To succeed with by-product synergy, good communication among all project stakeholders – business, communities and government agencies – is essential.

Even if they are not direct partners in the project, affected communities and government agencies should be recognized as vital stakeholders and therefore included in communications. This will help the efforts proceed more quickly and overcome barriers to success.

☐ Innovation

To overcome numerous barriers to by-product synergy projects, innovation is often required, from the invention of new conversion technologies to the creation of strategies for overcoming regulatory disincentives and other barriers.

☐ Participation

Successful by-product synergy requires active participation throughout the collaborating organizations, from CEO to factory-floor worker, community leader to citizen. All organizational levels should be involved in identifying, evaluating and implementing the project to ensure that all potential barriers to success are identified and overcome.

☐ Evaluation

A by-product synergy project must be evaluated throughout its life-cycle – before during and after implementation – to ensure that the economic, environmental and social objectives of the project are being achieved. If not, corrective action must be taken.

■ SDX Checklist for Eco-Efficiency[71]

■ MATERIAL INTENSITY

❑ Can the product or service be redesigned to make less use of material inputs?

❑ Are there less material-intensive raw materials?

❑ Can raw materials be produced or processed in less material-intensive ways?

❑ Would higher-quality materials create less waste in later stages?

❑ Can water, waste water treatment or waste disposal costs be allocated to budgets to encourage greater control?

❑ Can yields be increased by better maintenance, control or other means?

❑ Can waste be utilized?

❑ Can products be made of smaller size, or a different shape, to minimize material and packaging requirements?

❑ Can it be combined with others to reduce overall material intensity?

❑ Can packaging be eliminated or reduced?

■ ENERGY

❑ Can raw materials be produced with less, or renewable, energy?

❑ Would substitute materials or components reduce the overall energy intensity?

❑ Can energy costs be directly allocated to budgets to encourage better control?

❑ Can energy be exchanged between processes? Can waste heat be utilized?

❑ Can processes be integrated to create energy savings?

❑ Can process energy or the energy consumption of buildings be better monitored?

❑ Could better maintenance improve energy efficiency?

❑ Can processes or buildings be insulated more effectively?

❑ Is there scope for better energy housekeeping, such as energy-efficiency lighting?

❑ Can the product or services be combined with others to reduce overall energy intensity?

❑ Can the energy efficiency of products in use be improved?

❑ Can transport be reduced or greater use be made of energy-efficient transport?

❑ Are there incentives for employees to cycle or to use public transport or car pools?

■ TOXIC DISPERSION

❑ Can toxic dispersion be reduced or eliminated by using alternative raw materials or producing them differently?

❑ Are products designed to ensure their safe distribution, use and disposal?

❑ Can harmful substances be eliminated from production processes?

❑ Can harmful substances generated in use be reduced or eliminated?

❑ Can any remaining harmful substances be recycled or incinerated?

❑ Are remaining harmful substances properly handled during production and disposal?

❑ Are equipment and vehicles properly maintained so that emissions are kept to a minimum?

■ RECYCLABILITY

❑ Can the product be re-used, remanufactured or recycled?

❑ Can wastes from raw material production be re-used or recycled?

❑ Can process waste be remanufactured, re-used or recycled?

❑ Would separation of waste streams make recycling easier or reduce cost?

❑ Can product specification be modified to enable greater use of recycled materials or components?

❑ Can products be made of marked and easily recyclable materials?

❑ Can products be designed to facilitate customer revalorization?

❑ Can products be designed for easy disassembly?

❑ Can product packaging be made more recyclable?

❑ Can old products and components be remanufactured or re-used?

❑ Are there opportunities to participate in waste exchange schemes?

❑ Can products be made biodegradable or harmless so that less energy is required for disposal?

■ RESOURCES

❑ Can renewable or abundant materials be substituted for scarce or non-renewable ones?

❑ Can more use be made of resources that are certified as being sustainably produced?

❑ Can products be designed to utilize renewable or abundant materials?

■ DURABILITY

❑ Can materials or processes be altered in order to improve longevity?

❑ Can products or components be made more modular to allow easy upgrading?

❑ Can whatever aspects of the products that limit durability be redesigned?

❑ Can maintenance of the product be improved?

❑ Can customers be informed about ways to extending product durability?

■ SERVICE INTENSITY

❑ What service are customers really getting from your product?

❑ Can this be provided more effectively or in a completely different way?

❑ What service will customers need in the future?

❑ Can you design new or develop existing products to meet them?

❑ Is your product improving other services as well as the most obvious one?

❑ Can it be integrated/synchronized with others to provide multifunctionality?

❑ Can customers disposal problems be eliminated by providing a take-back service?

❑ Can production be localized both to enhance service and reduce transport needs?

Sustainable Shareholder Value

inter-office memorandum **sdx**

To:	Peter Kennedy, CEO <ptk>
From:	Li Cheng, VP, Corporate Finance <lc>
Date:	June 12, 2000
Subject:	Financial challenges of sustainable development

The economic aspects of sustainable development will in future be at the core of new business managers' thinking. We shall have to wrestle with questions such as: What is the cost of investment decisions, of environmental liabilities, or insurance implications? How will sustainable development affect the bottom-line?

A growing range of environmental issues can have an impact on a company's **profit and loss account** through:

- Revenue effects associated with market growth or decline
- Costs of clean-up expenditures or fines for non-compliance
- Insurance coverage
- R&D programs to stay ahead of rules and regulations

Likewise they can affect a company's **balance sheet** via:

- Land revaluations
- Plant write-offs
- Changes in the net realizable value of stock
- Liabilities (via remediation requirements)

The banking and insurance sector, and other players in the financial community, are today paying increasing attention to environmental issues and they are likely to become a major force in making companies look more closely at the link between environment and the financial performance.[72]

The chief financial officers in many companies are already taking a second look at sustainable development issues to find out the effect they may have on both shareholder value and the cost of operations.

Policy responses:
Some governments are already planning to make environmental information more systematically visible to the stock market. For example:

- In the U.S., the Security and Exchange Commission makes a greater demand for information disclosure from publicly listed companies. Together with other regulatory disclosure requirements, such as the Toxic Release Inventory (TRI), this means that U.S. analysts have traditionally had better access to information related to listed companies.

- The Swedish Government is working on guidelines for the reporting of environmental performance by Swedish companies quoted on the Stockholm stock exchange.
- Similar disclosure requirements are being discussed in most countries of the European Union.

Why is this important for our business?

A recent report by the WBCSD[73] showed that "environmental drivers," by which is meant the actions taken by companies to improve their environmental performance, can provide clear competitive advantages.

The report said that more and more companies, regardless of their size, sector or country of origin, are beginning to use environmental drivers as a means of enhancing their short- and long-term performance.

As a consequence, investment firms are starting to research these drivers as one the elements in their financial analysis of companies

What would encourage corporate financial officers to look more closely at the sustainable development opportunities and risks? To mention but one compelling reason cited in the WBCSD study: it can reduce the cost of credit.

All banks nowadays routinely look at the environmental performance of a borrower and may offer better rates to borrowers that can show a good environmental record. Admittedly, it is still more common for a borrower to be penalized for having a shaky environmental performance than to be rewarded for having a good one. Nevertheless, a growing number of financial institutions are coming to recognize that it is not just a case of evaluating the downside risk of an investment, but also the upside of a better-managed company

> *For example, CIBA, the pharmaceuticals and chemicals group (now split into Ciba Chemicals and Novartis), quantified the total financial value of two of its business units with and without environmental strategies, to evaluate whether environmentally-induced cash outflows increased or decreased the financial value of the business units. It found that a proactive strategy of environmental investments, despite an initial increase in cash outflows, led to a higher financial value.*

One thing is clear: environmental investment issues should not be relegated to the margins of the financial world. By scrutinizing them like any other investment proposal, sustainable development will move into mainstream consideration, in the same way that quality did in the past.

Li Cheng

To: All Financial Sector and Investor Relations staff
From: Vice-President, Corporate Finance

SDX Policy on Sustainable Shareholder Value

Commercial bankers, particularly in the industrial world, have begun to respond to the sustainable development agenda. This will have a direct impact on our relations with the financial sector.

When **lending,** banks are increasingly refining their credit approval by assessing environmental risks beyond, for example, contaminated sites.

In order to meet these requirements, a growing number of companies are moving from simply describing their environmental performance by reporting positive stories to assessing their eco-efficiency and the impact of environmental risks on their financial performance.

In **asset management,** leading institutions, such as the Swiss Bank Corporation, have developed specialized Environmental Performance Rating Units whose task it is to improve the quality of the financial analysis of a company by including environmental criteria in the process.

Analysts have traditionally made their forecasts of earnings-per-share, revenues, etc. using well-understood concepts based on accounting and similar rules. However, other, "softer," less-easy-to-quantify factors such as reputation, brand loyalty and quality of management are also taken into account. Today, environmental competence and the potential for eco-efficiency are increasingly being added to the mix.

Why is this important for our business?

The methods used to take advantage of environmental drivers naturally vary from company to company, but some general principles may be formulated that are also relevant for evaluating our company.

For example, Kværner, a leading international engineering company, secured funding for a revolving credit facility of several hundred million U.S. dollars in 1995 at a rate that was "a few basis points" cheaper than the standard rate. The reason was said, in part, to be the company's environmental performance.[74]

These general principles hold true, whether one is talking of "value-oriented" investors armed with calculational methods, or "growth-oriented" investors who take a more qualitative view, or indeed those who fall between the two extremes.

Those who are able to rate the eco-efficiency of a customer will have two important trump cards in their hands... first, they will own a credit portfolio with higher quality customers... second, they will be able to offer very competitive conditions by assessing the customer's risk. To a borrower, this means getting money on better terms.

Georges Blum, Chairman,
Swiss Bank Corporation

A few members of the WBCSD have pioneered methods for scrutinizing corporate eco-efficiency performance and linking them to a financial evaluation. One was Storebrand, which, with Scudder, launched an Environmental Value Fund in 1996. The fund invests in companies that rank among the top one-third in environmental performance within their industry sector.

The investment proposition is that, by performing an environmental screening upon a list of prime investment grade global companies, the resulting portfolio will provide investment value-added with higher returns than without the environmental screening. The first year's results showed clearly a consistently better performance than the reference index. Most importantly, it performed on average two percentage points better than the already well-performing Scudder fund from which it drew its potential investments. And it showed to be sturdier against downside fluctuations during the financial turmoil in late 1997.

We at SDX want to be part of such a selection. So, what do we have to do to be rated as one of the environmental "stars"?

The WBCSD's report, *Environmental Performance and Shareholder Value*, suggests typical questions which potential lenders or investors might ask a company under scrutiny. These are therefore questions that all of us at SDX must address:

1. Which environmental factors are financially relevant for this business?
2. What is the management's level of awareness of environmental drivers, and how well positioned is the company to take full advantage of them?
3. Are the environmental factors vulnerabilities for the business, or do they offer opportunities for its value-chain?
4. Is there a management system in place on matters such as policy, goals, programs and actions to record and evaluate environmental data and to ensure follow-up, where necessary?
5. Where and how is that system put into practice (R&D, manufacturing, sales-marketing, legal, lobbying, accruals, etc.)?
6. When and how do environmental drivers hit the bottom-line, and what are reasonable expectations?

These are important questions and we must think about them carefully. Accordingly, once the summer vacation period is over, I plan to arrange a one-day workshop for all Stakeholder Relations staff so that we can formulate our answers to them.

Li Cheng
July 6, 2000

Star Alliances and Partnerships

inter-office memorandum

To: Peter Kennedy <ptk>   cc   Strategy Review Group

From: Piotr Kalinskij, Manager, Stakeholder Relations <pvk>

Date: August 3, 2000

Subject: **How useful are alliances and partnerships?**

In advance of your forthcoming meeting with representatives of the Community Action Group, this memo aims to provide an overview of partnerships and their possible benefits.

1. Partnerships with governments

The past decade has seen a swing away from prescriptive legal controls on industry towards voluntary agreements between governments and industry. These agreements take many forms. For example:

- The **Dutch** have had considerable success with legally binding negotiated agreements (called *covenants*) established in particular industry sectors, where commitments are made to reduce emissions and improve environmental performance.

- The **European Union** is using this approach as a model to encourage what it calls "environmental agreements" throughout the EU. In 1995, the EU completed a study on ways to reduce exhaust emissions from cars. The fuel and the automotive industries both participated and, although this did not prevent disagreements between the two sectors, progress was made in setting targets and apportioning responsibility.

- The **United States** has a long record of experimenting with voluntary models. The Environmental Protection Agency (EPA) has started some 50 voluntary partnership programs in different industry sectors to encourage the reduction of emissions and wastes and to devise more environmentally efficient products. Some examples:
    - The so-called **33/50** program is designed to reduce toxic-waste generation.
    - The **Green Lights** program encourages voluntary reductions in energy use through energy-efficient lighting, resulting in reductions in carbon dioxide emissions.
    - In the **Design for Environment** program, the EPA works with the dry-cleaning, printing and electronics industries to reduce emissions.
    - The **Energy Star** program involves the computer industry in a drive to encourage energy efficiency in computer and electronic office products.
    - The **Waste Wise** program is designed to reduce solid wastes sent to landfills.

Another model of partnership has developed between UN agencies and business. In 1992, 30 leading banks signed a UNEP statement, and have since then worked with UNEP on voluntary environmental programs. A similar partnership was later established between UNEP and the insurance sector.

... August 3rd, 2000 ...

Why are partnerships important for business?

Business experience suggests that **voluntary agreements**, or **negotiated agreements**, as they are often called, reach commonly stated goals more effectively than regulations imposed by diktat.

Voluntary agreements are semi-formal or contractual arrangements between the regulatory authorities and industry sectors to achieve clearly defined goals within a certain time. Because voluntary agreements require an open dialogue about goals and priorities from the outset, and are built up in a spirit of partnership, they are more likely to succeed.

The key idea behind them is to set and then allow companies to devise their own strategies and choose their own technologies to reach the goals.

The principles for these agreements are simple:

- The authorities set up the framework and agree achievable but challenging targets jointly with the other stakeholders, including industry. Industry is then free to choose how to attain those targets.

- The agreement is voluntary, but if industry does not comply, the targets can be converted into commands through legislation.

- Companies find this preferable to laws that prescribe the methods and technologies to be used rather than encouraging industry to devise its own innovative approaches to such matters as waste reduction.

We have achieved average returns of 55 percent from voluntary, not compliance-driven, investments over the past 10 years and can thus expect continued financial gains from environmental performance improvements and from associated capital investments.

David T. Buzzelli
when Corporate Director of The Dow Chemical Company

---

2. Social partnerships

Business has traditionally found it difficult to co-operate with its critics or follow the lead of organizations outside government.

But the obvious change in corporate mood that followed the Rio Earth Summit in 1992 encouraged an unprecedented degree of exploration to find — through partnership — new solutions to some of the world's old environmental problems.

Partnership approaches have been on the agenda throughout the 1990s, but were given a major push forward by Agenda 21, one of the key outputs of the 1992 Earth Summit.

Through the implementation of growing numbers of local Agenda 21 initiatives, a great deal of progress is being made. The challenge is to pick the right projects and support them in the right way, without over-burdening the company's own resources.

Business must recognize that there is growing stakeholder awareness that business decisions are skewed when environmental performance, costs, and liabilities are not integrated into the strategic decision-making of our companies.

Allan Kupcis
former President and CEO, Ontario Hydro

Many companies believe that the **social license to operate** will become the third key issue (in addition to the economic and ecological dimensions) that board members will have to take account of when steering their company.

It therefore becomes important to integrate the commitment to environment and development into a corporation's social fabric.

Most large companies have a program for charitable giving and sponsorship of worthy causes, and increasingly these programs contain a budget designed to support not-for-profit environmental activities.

But, increasingly, companies are trying to evolve ways of using their people, management skills and technology, rather than simply their money, to help develop sustainability initiatives.

BankAmerica is one of the companies that has done a good deal to involve employees not only with its internal environmental programs but also with external activities. The bank's TeamAmerica, which co-ordinates all employee volunteer activities, made a special effort to include environmental initiatives in its program. During 1994 alone, some 50 events took place, involving more than 1,000 employees, their families and guests. The major event was "International Coastal Clean-Up," in which more than 600 employees and guests took part.

The leading edge

Several companies have taken the partnership concept further. I like to call these initiatives 'star alliances', as they often involve different stakeholders working co-operatively together. Examples include:

- S.C. Johnson Wax has formed the Alliance for Environmental Innovation with the U.S. Environmental Defense Fund and the Pew Foundation. A joint task force is working on the company's product formulation and packaging processes.[75]

- Dow Chemical is starting a new collaborative process with the U.S. Natural Resources Defense Council (NRDC) and the community. The aim is to help Dow achieve its corporate waste and emission reductions goals at a large manufacturing facility near its corporate headquarters in Midland, Michigan, U.S.A. This initiative will use a third-party pollution-prevention auditor, who will work with employees to identify and evaluate pollution prevention opportunities.

A similar pattern of partnerships is beginning to be seen in some of the developing countries:

- In South Africa, Eskom provides more than 95% of the country's electricity. The company believes that the provision of electricity "has social, economic and environmental benefits," giving it a strong "triple bottom-line" performance from the outset.

But the generation and supply of electrical power causes major environmental problems, too, even if it does bring benefits that are desperately needed by communities across the country. Eskom has therefore emerged as a pioneer in southern Africa in such areas as environmental impact assessment and in the consultation of communities at town or regional level — through the establishment of local community forums.

I believe it is clear from all the above that partnerships, both with governments and with other stakeholders in the community, offer the best prospect of achieving SDX's aims while advancing the cause of sustainable development.

P.Z. Kalinskij

SECTION SIX

Tools for Managing the Sustainable Corporation

> *The problems we have today cannot be solved by thinking the way we thought when we created them.*
>
> Albert Einstein

'GOOD TOOLS ARE HALF THE JOB.' That is true both for the craftsman and the manager of a business operation. We also want to share with you how the leading-edge companies are managing their operations in practical terms towards sustainability with the following tools.

▶ *Environmental Management Systems*

What is ISO 14001 all about? Does it set specific environmental performance levels? Does it require third-party verification?

▶ *Life-Cycle Assessment*

Is this a management system or an engineering discipline? Why is the use of targets, defined in regular reports, so important for regulators and campaigners?

▶ *Design for Environment (DFE)*

Is DFE focused on recycling or on remanufacturing? What is Design for Recycling (DFR) and Design for Disassembly (DFD)? Should one broaden the DFE concept to include product recovery and recycling strategies at the end of product life?

▶ *Remanufacturing or Dematerialisation?*

You can give products multiple life-cycles through remanufacturing — building or rebuilding products using 'second-hand' components. Is this strategy opposing the goal of dematerialisation, i.e providing the same service with less resource throughput?

▶ *Accounting for the Environment*

How widely is this approach accepted? What are the stumbling blocks today? What are the benchmarks for both internal and external techniques?

▶ *Environmental Reporting*

'Don't trust us, track us' was business's response to its critics, and in fulfilment of this, hundreds of companies worldwide are now producing annual environmental reports. Are they useful?

▶ *Closed-Loop Manufacturing Processes*

Are they feasible today? Does it pay to do it? What is by-product synergy?

▶ *Supply-Chain Auditing*

How do you apply your environmental standards to your suppliers? Are you responsible for their performance?

Peter Kennedy
Chief Executive Officer

To : New members of the *Sustainability 21* Program

Date   October 11, 2000

Subject:

How will we manage the sustainable corporation?

First of all, may I offer a heartfelt welcome to SDX Corporation and congratulate you for being one of only twenty candidates selected for SDX's *Sustainability 21 Program*. This program offers its successful candidates training experience in most of SDX's key departments, on a rotational basis. *Sustainability 21* will expose you to all practical aspects of Sustainability at SDX

In order to be a cutting-edge company in the new millennium, SDX needs a environmentally aware staff who understand what we have called the "Triple Bottom-Line." We want to run SDX as a leading example of a sustainable corporation. What does this mean to all of us?

One thing is clear: managing our corporation will require that you are familiar with the right management tools. Fortunately, we are not alone. Other leading companies have already looked into what it will take to run a successful business in the next century; and new management concepts and tools are emerging.

I have therefore asked Jacques Perrier, our management education advisor, to identify these new management tools for you, to explain how we are using them and why they are becoming increasingly important, and to zero in on a few companies that are also operating at the "cutting edge."

These tools are there to help you perform professionally and help steer SDX well into the next century.

Peter Kennedy

... October 11th, 2000 ...

■ Environmental Management Systems

■ The tool

Like many companies that began to report on their environmental performance, SDX found their internal environmental management systems (EMSs) were not up to the task. As a result, we have seen growing interest in the development of national and international EMS standards.

Now, after the pioneering work of the British Standards Institution (which developed BS 7750, the first environmental management systems standard) and initiatives by Frank Bosshardt and members of the World Business Council for Sustainable Development, a range of EMS standards have emerged through the **International Organization for Standardization**. They are called the ISO 14000 series.

In 1996, the main international EMS standard – **ISO 14001** – was published worldwide. Developed over five years, with inputs from a wide spectrum of experts, the standard is designed to help organizations manage their impact on the environment, no matter what their size, nature or location.[76]

The standards do not set specific environmental performance levels such as emission levels. Instead they use a management-system approach similar to the earlier ISO 9000 quality standards.

Registered companies are regularly scrutinized by accredited auditors and are not allowed to use the ISO symbol unless their management system conforms to the standard. The ISO 14000 standards are attracting wide interest around the world. The series consists of five primary standards covering:

- **Environmental auditing**
- **Environmental labeling**
- **Environmental performance evaluation**
- **Life-cycle assessment**
- **Environmental management systems**

The ISO standard does not require the report produced by the company to be verified externally. Moreover, applying for accreditation is voluntary and to a great extent market-driven. Most companies that conform to the standards argue that they become more competitive as a result of conforming and being accredited.

Certification operates at the level of the *whole business unit.* So, for example, ABB Asea Brown Boveri's 1996 environmental report noted that 50 ABB companies had at that time been certified under ISO 14001. Today, a total of 250 ABB companies are implementing ISO 14001.

In Europe, the **Eco-Management and Auditing Scheme (EMAS)** has been developed on the initiative of the European Commission. This, too, operates on a voluntary basis, with registration at the site level.

It was developed originally for large industrial sites but is now compatible with the ISO 14000 series and it can be used by smaller companies.

The main difference between ISO 14000 and EMAS is that EMAS includes a **performance evaluation**, resulting in an annual **public environmental statement** after the company has been reviewed and audited by independent verifiers.

The EU is currently considering extending EMAS to cover service industries, such as banks.

A board of directors unconcerned with standards will not find itself at the head of a successful company for long. Relevant and appropriate standards are essential throughout any business. They are all about efficiency and competitiveness. They help to achieve "fit for purpose" performance, reliability, and consistency. They ensure the safety of employees and the public, and have an important role in protecting the environment.

Ed Wallis, Chairman, PowerGen

Critics of ISO 14000 argue that the standards do not improve performance but merely require conformity with a management system. On the other hand, it is hard to see how, in the absence of any well-defined management concept, progress in environmental management can be measured.

■ The Life-Cycle Approach

Life-cycle analysis (LCA), also called life-cycle assessment, is a key element in SDX's environmental management approach.

In its simplest form, LCA involves listing the various positive and negative environmental aspects of a specific product throughout its life-cycle.

The life-cycle approach can change the way products are made, packaged, transported, sold, used, re-used, recycled and disposed of. It can also result in the development of entirely new products and services. More and more companies are using the developing science of LCA as a tool to reduce the overall effect their products and production processes have on the environment.

The information can be useful at the design (or redesign) stage of a product. It indicates what aspects, such as the source of raw materials, could be changed or eliminated in order to improve the product's overall environmental performance.

> *At Xerox, where managing by data and facts is fundamental, the LCA has provided the information necessary to quantify areas where the greatest improvements can be made. Our experience shows that simple LCAs can provide value in research, technology, and design decision-making.*
>
> **Paul A. Allaire, Chairman and CEO, Xerox Corporation**

LCA, while useful, can be both expensive and difficult:

- Listing the various environmental pros and cons of, say, a packaging material can involve collecting thousands of different bits of information from various sources.

- Some information is often just not available.

- Judging a product's or a service's merits and demerits can prove difficult – some would say impossible – without a universally agreed frame of reference to weight the various attributes.

Despite these difficulties, some companies, such as Procter & Gamble, have made extensive use of the technique and have, with others, funded its development through the Society for the Promotion of LCA Development.

Furthermore, LCA is but one technical tool among several, although the concept of considering a product's life-cycle is broadly applicable in all of them.

■ Why is LCA important for business?

Many companies feel their own environmental management systems and standards are already sufficiently rigorous, and that this makes it unnecessary for them to conform with independent standards.

But conformance with the standards will signal a high level of management quality. Some companies believe this may release them from regular and expensive monitoring by the authorities. As with Total Quality Management (TQM) standards, however, organizations can develop world-class management systems, yet make little real progress. This is why the use of targets and the production of regular reports are seen as important by many regulators and campaigners.

■ Companies at the cutting edge

A growing number of companies provide details of their environmental management systems in their reports. Most of them are manufacturing companies. They include Dow Europe, Novo Nordisk, Procter & Gamble, Unilever and Xerox. But these companies are now being joined by a range of service, retailing, distribution and, increasingly, financial companies.

Often, the most interesting reports are those produced by companies straddling a range of different industry sectors.

For example, Canada's Noranda is a diversified natural resources company operating in three sectors: mining and metals, forest products, and oil and gas. Noranda's 1995 Environment, Health and Safety Report accounted for 38 environmental, health and safety audits carried out at 18 wholly-owned operations.[77] The report said that the company's mining and milling operations had achieved their target of reducing metals discharged into water by 75% from 1990 levels; and that Noranda Aluminum had cut its chlorine use by 75% over the same period.

■ Sustainability and Design: DFE

■ The tools

For SDX, *Designing for Sustainability* is at the core of achieving eco-efficiency. The basis is Design for the Environment (DFE), which includes a set of evolving tools for designing, engineering and manufacturing products with an improved environmental performance throughout their life-cycle.

The DFE approach is straightforward: systematically examine a product from "cradle to grave" and then introduce changes to improve its overall environmental performance.

Two key developments in recent years have had a profound effect on the emergence of DFE principles and practices: first, the introduction of eco-labels, and second, legislation that requires manufacturers to recover and recycle products at the end of their useful life.

The origins of DFE can be traced to a specific engineering design approach, Design for "X" (DFX). In this procedure, "X" represents any product characteristic such as manufacturability, reliability, or in this case, "E" for environment, that a company wants to maximize in its product design. Some examples:

- In AT&T and other companies that employ the DFX approach, DFE can refer literally to the integration of environmental issues into their design procedure.

- Variations depend on a company's environmental objectives. Hitachi, for example, focuses on Design for Recycling (DFR) and Design for Disassembly (DFD).

- Xerox broadens the DFE concept to include product recovery and recycling strategies at the end of product life.

- Similarly, at AT&T, DFE is a component of what it calls "Green Product Realization," a process to improve the environmental performance throughout the product's life.

■ Why is DFE important for business?

DFE activities are aimed at achieving better market positioning, lower costs and a greater degree of managerial control by being "ahead of the regulator."

Environmental credentials are an essential part of market positioning for many companies. We carried out an informal survey of a number of companies known to have adopted a DFE approach and they said its benefits include:

- A small, but not yet decisive, market edge, created by environmental merit. In the long term, we believe additional weight should be given to the "environmental merit" factor.

- Strengthened company reputation. DFE demonstrates that environmental considerations are high on the company's agenda and that the company has made a long-term commitment to improved environmental performance.

- Increased awareness within the company of the environmental impact of its products and processes. It sends a powerful message to employees and may well result in better morale and higher productivity.

■ Companies at the cutting edge

There is little point in producing environmentally sensitive solutions if the resulting products are too expensive, inconvenient or unattractive for anyone to want to buy and use. But designing for minimal environmental impact need not produce drab, poor-quality products that give satisfaction only through "guilt-reduction."[78]

Xerox, for example, says it is aiming "to produce waste-free products in waste-free factories." In its 1995 report,[79] the company says DFE now influences not only how its products are designed, but also what happens to them at the end of their initial life-cycle.

A majority of manufacturing companies see DFE as being a major contributor to their future success saying that business opportunities and environmental benefits have already resulted from their efforts.

Factors that are influencing the trend include:

- Manufacturers are responding to a greater demand from customers for products that have less effect on the environment as well as to stipulations by customers that they, the manufacturers, take products back for recycling or disposal.

- Reduced environmental releases, chemical use and waste generation, which can diminish a company's regulatory and tax burdens and liability. For instance, Norwegian oil company Statoil says that DFE provides it with an opportunity to reduce its tax burden by lowering its process emissions.

- Improved overall product performance per unit price. Kodak and Hitachi have both found that many products designed on DFE principles perform better than competing products.

- Retail establishments are placing similar demands on manufacturers to reduce costs, including those relating to production, inventory, raw materials and waste disposal. This is most clearly the case when design changes reduce the requirement for resources such as raw materials and energy or when they cut waste production or ensure that components can be re-used many times. For example, Xerox says it cut its unit manufacturing costs by means of its program to recover and recycle product components after customers had finished with them.

■ A DFE toolbox

We set out below a number of elements that we consider together make up a useful "toolbox" for any company embarking on DFE.

☐ Design guidelines

Common to most DFE programs is the development of DFE design manuals to inform and guide the decisions of design staff. As well as setting out general design guidelines, these manuals often provide the rationale for undertaking DFE initiatives, including corporate policies and legislative influences.

BMW and SIEMENS have produced environmental guides for product development that cover choice of materials, number and composition of components, component labeling, design for disassembly and re-use of materials. Subsequently, the companies will incorporate corporate guidelines into business unit-specific design guides.

☐ Materials and chemical lists

Some companies provide design engineers with lists of restricted and acceptable materials or chemicals for use in the company's operations or in the components it purchases.

Materials classification are based on factors such as legal restrictions, toxicity and recyclability. At some companies (Philips, for example), materials and components are also given scores for their degree of "environmental release" relative to other materials. These scores are subsequently used in the development of overall "green" design scores.

☐ Design reviews

Some companies require standardized environmental checklists to be completed as part of the formal product development process. Checklists usually take the form of a series of questions appropriate to the product development phase. Questions such as "What do customers require?" or "Are restricted chemicals used to make the product?" might be asked in the product planning and product design stages, respectively.

At designated points in the formal process of product review, managers can evaluate and approve the checklists, along with other product documentation. As with any other design criterion, failure to meet environmental design requirements can result in rejection of the design, or a delay in the product's development cycle.

At HITACHI, special committees oversee each company design to assess whether it complies with the company's policies and makes a contribution to its targets on recycling.

☐ Product development planning documents

In addition to design reviews, product planning documentation may include environmental impact assessments and recycling plans.

IBM requires its product development teams, as an early task in the development process, to assess and record the environmental impact of new products and processes throughout their life-cycle. Similarly, IBM and Xerox require the development of a re-use and recycling strategy document.

☐ Analytical tools

Several types of analytical tool are being developed to support design decisions and measure product life-cycle performance. A WBCSD study found three distinct tools: Life-Cycle Assessment (LCA), "Green" scoring systems, and Life-Cycle Costing.

Common to each of these methods is a life-cycle approach. To assist design engineers in the execution of these complex analyzes and to provide consistency in their application, computer software tools are under development.

AT&T has developed a "green" scoring system that rates the overall environmental performance of a product. Green design rules, based on experience and intuition, form the basis of the company's scoring system.

Numerous companies and government agencies are developing specific LCA methodologies and tools to guide environmentally sound product development.

VOLVO has led a collaborative effort among Swedish scientists and industry to develop a methodology called the EPS system (Environmental Priority Strategies in product design). EPS aims to provide a thorough life-cycle approach within realistic cost and time constraints

---

Remanufacturing or Dematerialization?

Planning for remanufacturing

Increasingly, companies aim to give products multiple life-cycles through remanufacturing – a process that entails building or rebuilding products using "second-hand" components. At the end of the process, the products should meet the same high quality standards as their new counterparts.

At present, the remanufacturing challenge is harder to meet than it will be in the future. This is because most of the products coming back today were not designed with remanufacturing or even recycling in mind.

Some companies, computer manufacturer Compaq for example, are now using DFE and life-cycle assessment tools to ensure that new products are much easier to remanufacture.

The rate of progress is shown by the following example. In 1994, 25% of Xerox's new product programs included environmental features; by 1995 the figure had increased to 70%. Xerox made savings of several hundred million dollars from this in 1995 alone.

Dematerialization and resource-productivity

Western societies historically have not generally encouraged serviceability and longevity in product design criteria. As a result, resource-productivity is low and overall use of resources is high. Resource-productivity is a very useful concept since it helps us distinguish between the different strategies that we might use to improve the ratio between resource use and the production of useful goods and services. There are two main efficiency strategies: reducing the resource-intensity of products and processes (dematerialization), and increasing the functionality and serviceability of products. Prof. Ulrich von Weizsäcker (with Amory and Hunter Lovins), taking mid-1990s efficiency levels as a benchmark (Schmidt-Bleek's "factor" concept), has argued that, using current best available technologies and approaches, an aggregate **Factor 4** improvement on today's resource-productivity is achievable.[80]

For companies, this means rethinking even more dramatically what service a product is suppose to deliver, and it requires a strong eco-innovation approach to product design at a very early stage.

Towards Factor 10

However, von Weizsäcker *et al.* acknowledge that, because of predicted population growth and increased worldwide consumption levels, even if this Factor 4 revolution were achieved from 1995 to 2050, any efficiency gains would be cancelled out. Friedrich Schmidt-Bleek and the members of the "Factor 10 Club", a group of leading international figures in environment and development, therefore propose a more ambitious approach.[81]

They argue that the inequities of living standards and access to resources between richer countries and developing nations needs to be taken into account. Around four-fifths of all presently used resources are used by the richest fifth of the world's population. The inevitable development and population growth of the poorer nations will have a huge bearing on the demand for resources in the next fifty years. Therefore, all the required absolute reduction in resource use will have to come from the richer nations. This argues the need for a **Factor 10** (or higher) improvement in resource productivity in the developed world.

This has important implications.

- New technologies must be developed.

- Structural changes to society. A shift is required from a wealth-seeking, production-oriented society that seeks increasing returns from labor to a society that emphasizes conservation and seeks increasing returns from resources.

- We must begin immediately.

■ Accounting for the Environment

■ The concept

SDX feels that environmental accounting is still at an early stage in its development, but new approaches to both financial and non-financial reporting are now evolving rapidly. There is a rising interest on two different levels – national and corporate. The aims are:

- To revise the **national accounts** in order to produce a better instrument for steering the economy.

- To expand **corporate accounts** to reflect the company's handling of its environmental and social assets.

Let us look at each of these in turn.

☐ Revising national accounts

The national accounting system may not at first sight be of direct relevance to companies. However, it can give a company's management important indicators of the health of the business climate around the world. Companies will therefore be better served if the accuracy of national accounts in sustainable development terms is improved.

Currently, Gross Domestic Product (GDP) – an indicator of economic health – rises when costs are incurred in repairing damage from disasters. The World Wide Fund for Nature (WWF) is therefore pressing for national indicators, such as GDP, to reflect *environmental degradation.*

The Green Gross Domestic Product is defined as the Net National Product minus the Depreciation of its Natural Capital.

UN Handbook

☐ Expanding corporate accounts

Recently there has been a significant shift in attitude towards accounting for environmental issues. Some trends:

- The pressure to put a financial figure on what society values – a cleaner environment, for example – is beginning to register within accounting circles, especially with increasing demands from the investment community to identify those business risks that are environmentally determined.

- Some companies have made progress in identifying their environmental costs clearly. These costs are generally carried as an overhead but are now starting to be allocated to particular production processes.

- These companies have found that identifying the extent of their environmental costs – by specific accounting methods – can help in decisions about the viability of products.

The history of accounting practice, however, shows that it could be a difficult and slow process to get new standards accepted.[82]

Green Ledgers, a study by the World Resources Institute published in 1995, showed that 22% of operating costs (excluding feedstock) at Amoco Oil's refinery at Yorktown in the U.S. were considered to be environmental. Also, about 2.4% of the net sales for consumer products at S.C. Johnson Wax were environmental, as were more than 19% of manufacturing costs for one of DuPont's agricultural pesticides.[83]

■ Policy responses

A number of policy responses to Accounting for the Environment are afoot. For example:

- The United Nations has taken some early steps towards proposing directions in the UN Initiative on External Environmental Reporting.

- The Scandinavian countries have started to experiment with elements of a satellite accounting system. Denmark, for example, has introduced a Law on Green Accounting.

- So far, the only concrete demands on companies to identify separately their environmental risks concern the current and future cost of decontaminating land and groundwater.

- Companies operating in the U.S. (as well as non-U.S. companies listed on U.S. stock exchanges) are required by the Securities and Exchange Commission to disclose environmental exposures that could affect their market value.

- The European Union's **Accounting Advisory Forum** is preparing an opinion on how to improve reporting on the environment in annual reports and accounts. Similar bodies are also working on a reform of standards to take account of the environment.

■ Environmental accounting and business

Accounting always provides an incomplete picture, given that it covers only those things that can be measured.[84] But even in conventional financial accounting practice, ways are being developed to ascribe a financial value to such corporate assets as reputation, brand and intellectual capital.

Increasingly, society will demand – and successful companies will use – accounting methods that capture at least part of the economic, environmental and social costs associated with production and consumption activities. The term **"full-cost accounting"** is sometimes used to describe this goal.

The importance of such accounts to corporate boards is clear. Unless company directors have clear, credible performance data, they will continue to find it difficult to assess the importance for their business of the different aspects of the sustainability agenda.

Our customers are starting to ask for more information about the environmental performance of investments in stocks. We feel sure that these trends will lead in the near future to standards that will make it easier to account for the full impact of environmental issues on financial performance.

Agreed common environmental performance and accounting standards have yet to emerge. This makes it difficult for both industry and the financial services sector to evaluate exactly the effect of environmental factors on financial performance.

Georges Blum, Chairman, Swiss Bank Corporation

Benchmarking is another area in which better environmental accounting will help. Member companies of the World Business Council for Sustainable Development (WBCSD) are now actively investigating this area.

A number of company reports now provide performance data that are linked to a unit of output. For example, in Shell UK's 1995 report, the unit adopted was "per barrel of oil produced." Other companies' reports, such as that produced by Anglian Water in the UK, compare the company's performance with sectoral averages.

■ Companies at the cutting edge

One of the first companies to include an early form of environmental accounting in its annual report was the Dutch management consultancy BSO/Origin. Instead of focusing on either the profit-and-loss account or the balance sheet, BSO/Origin concentrated on the value-added statement. The company noted that economic value can only be created at the cost of some environmental degradation. Its first statement, in 1990, included an essay entitled "Pulling our Planet out of the Red."

A different approach was that adopted by Danish Steel Works (Det Danske Stålvalseværk A/S) in its "Green Accounts." These were based on a mass balance sheet, showing all environmentally significant inputs and outputs from the company's operations. This approach helped catalyze Denmark's new national system of green accounts, now an annual requirement for more than 3,000 companies.

Among the companies referring to environmental cost accounting is General Motors.[85] Others – including Nortel (Canada), Novo Nordisk (Denmark) and SAS (Sweden) – are using their own **environmental performance indexes**.

These indexes pull together data on the company's performance against a range of indicators and then, potentially, provide an overall aggregate figure for the latest year. The maximum score in Nortel's system, for example, would be 175 per annum. In its 1995 report, the company noted that its 1994 score was 136.[86]

Building on the recommendations of its book, *Financing Change*,[87] the WBCSD has recently published a report, *Environmental Performance and Shareholder Value*,[88] discussing how eco-efficient practices can create shareholder value.

The objective of the report is to help companies and investors alike to understand how to factor good environmental performance into any assessment of a company's long-term financial worth. A key recommendation is the need to develop indicators that account as objectively as possible for the environmental and sustainable development achievements of a company.

Storebrand, Norway's leading private-sector supplier of financial and insurance services, and Scudder, Stevens & Clark, one of America's oldest and largest investment management firms, have developed their own "Sustainability Index," as have banks such as the Swiss Bank Corporation.

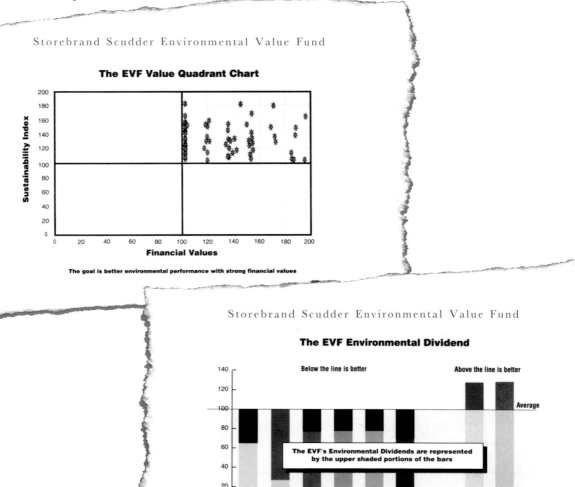

briefing notes for new managers

■ Environmental Reporting

■ Issues and trends

For SDX, corporate transparency is one critical step in the direction of greater accountability, credibility and trust. "Don't trust us, track us" was business's response to its critics, and, in fulfillment of this, hundreds of companies worldwide are now producing annual environmental reports, mostly on a voluntary basis.

Modeled very much on annual financial reports and accounts, these documents report on environmental issues and the company's attitude towards them, and provide data on a wide range of environmental performance parameters. Many include information and data on emissions, which allows outsiders to track the company's year-on-year performance.

These reports are part of the commitments that chemical companies undertake when signing up to the industry's Responsible Care® program.

Other companies in many other sectors have also started to report in this way. However, when the U.S. Investor Responsibility Research Center (IRRC) carried out its second survey of Standard & Poor 500 companies, measuring their performance against five key indicators, it found that relatively few companies could provide the data requested.[89]

Various broad-based standards have emerged to make the data more comparable across sectors and the reports more consistent in their content. Examples include the Public Environmental Reporting Initiative (PERI), the guidelines of the Coalition for Environmentally Responsible Economies (CERES) and those from the United Nations Environment Program (UNEP).

Critics argue that the information contained in the reports is of limited use because it is self-generated and self-published and has little, if any, third-party verification. They also contend that because the reporting standards, such as those of PERI and UNEP, are both broad and voluntary, it is difficult to compare the relative performance of companies, especially in different sectors.

However, to allow readers of the reports, and other stakeholders, to understand and measure the extent to which progress is being made, a growing number of companies are now beginning to publish **annual targets** in their reports.

■ What does Environmental Reporting offer to business?

Companies will have to deal with a growing variety of stakeholders. A constructive relationship with these groups must build on trust and understanding. Public reporting is a cornerstone for such trust.

The existence and success of these environmental reports has helped dispel the myth that it is unwise to lift the corporate head above the parapet. In fact, the reaction has tended to be just the reverse: companies that publish a report often complain that it gets *too little* attention.

As well as the extra public trust an environmental report may create, the very process of producing the report is also useful internally:

- It often helps companies get to grips with parts of their business that have not come under specific management scrutiny before.

- The process forces managers to focus on difficult issues that are sometimes easier to ignore. It can expose a lack of clear policy on such matters as global standards, animal testing, or business ethics.

- The reports have been successful in providing information on the more negative aspects of company performance, such as emissions of toxic waste, thus allowing the company to deal with them more effectively.

For many companies, the annual environmental report is fast becoming a source of information for customers who demand evidence on the environmental performance of their own supply-chain.

Investors, too, are looking to these reports for evidence of the effective management of environmental risk. However, as noted earlier, they often find the lack of benchmarking and reporting standards to be a handicap when trying to extract and interpret the particular information they need.

■ The dilemma

Companies have tended to start off with auditing, move on to reporting and, only now, are beginning to think about environmental accounting.

As more and more companies join the ranks of those publishing environmental reports, the very reporting itself remains haunted with something of a paradox.[90]

There is a difference between the way many companies *think* readers are using their reports and what is *actually happening.*

Many companies imagine that users are looking for a source of reassurance, best-practice examples and information for decision-making. The evidence suggests, however, that some of the more important stakeholder groups are now using the reported data for measuring, monitoring, screening, comparing and benchmarking.

Yet without greater standardization in reporting, many of these reports remain difficult to compare, and the underlying performance is difficult to benchmark.

These are challenges that report-makers and report-users alike will need to work on jointly in the future.

■ Where now?

Companies that have been reporting for some time are wrestling with the demand to measure more effectively their environmental impact. But progress *is* being made, especially on finding new ways to quantify the environmental relevance.

For example, the UK-based chemicals group, ICI, has introduced a system of measuring what it calls "Environmental Burden." This is an approach that reports on the impact of the group's activities and products in a way that reflects the way the chemical industry operates.

The next step, which several leading companies have already taken, is to report on **social issues.**

In these so-called "social reports" or "audits," companies cover such issues as employment practices, occupational health, civic involvement, land use, charitable donations and community action. They can be seen as providing evidence that business is beginning to acknowledge all three of the pillars of sustainable development: economic, environmental and social.

The reporting habit is spreading around the world. In Korea, for example, LG Semicon produced its first report, in English, in 1995.[91] The report speaks of stakeholder involvement.

Ultimately, we will witness the disappearance of the corporate environmental report and even, in time, the sustainable development report. We will know we are really changing course when one corporate annual report presents past performance and future goals integrating financial stewardship with environmental integrity and social responsibility.

Allan Kupcis, when President and CEO, Ontario Hydro

■ Closing the Manufacturing Processes Loop

■ The concept

Concern about the use of potentially hazardous and toxic materials (including genetically modified organisms) in manufacturing has led to the development of so-called "closed processes."

Closed Manufacturing Processes are systems designed to contain the process and insulate it from the environment. Key elements of the approach include:

- Optimizing resource productivity throughout the production process

- Screening out high-waste inputs

- Changing product design to allow production operations to push towards the target of "zero emissions"

A growing numbers of companies, among them Xerox and 3M with its pioneering "Pollution Prevention Pays" (3P) program, are coming to recognize the need to "close the loop" in their operations.

The paper industry is already moving towards closed bleaching processing systems, in which the effluent waters are recycled and not emitted to the environment. At least 15 mills worldwide – in Sweden, Canada, Finland, the U.S. and South Africa – are now implementing these closed-cycle bleaching processes.

> *We have realized over $20 million in annual cost-savings and reductions by cutting manufacturing waste in half and reducing virgin packaging use by 25 percent. 95 percent of wastewater from one of our plants is continuously reused – never to be discharged.*
>
> **Samuel C. Johnson Chairman, S.C. Johnson & Son**

■ Recycling and take-back schemes

The recycling of costly or *potentially hazardous substances* is now well established in many manufacturing industries.

For example, the Saturn division of General Motors in the United States has, since 1995, collected used and damaged plastic materials from its network of retailers. The collections are transported using the same delivery trucks that in the old days returned empty from retailers. The materials are then taken to a plastics reprocessing company for use in several automotive applications.

Environmental pressures have also led to innovation in the design of products in order to make them, or their components, more easily recyclable. However, a big task for business is to devise **take-back** schemes for products or materials that have little value – packaging material, for instance.

Considerable progress has already been made in reducing the volume and weight of packaging, as well as in working with waste-disposal authorities to organize recycling schemes. But there is a need to establish a suitable infrastructure and the right market conditions to make the exercise economically viable.

■ Why is Closed Manufacturing important for business?

Because of the increasing cost of handling waste in an environmentally sensitive manner, and with growing pressure on companies' costs, sustainable development requires massive improvements in resource productivity in every sector of industry.

This will entail integrating the techniques of eco-efficiency, environmental management systems, environmental accounting and design for the environment into the production plant by closing the loops.

☐ Closing the larger loops

One opportunity for companies is to integrate their processes with those of other corporations. Industrial parks, where one company's useful wastes are used by a neighbor, could reduce the overall level of waste and cut the cost of waste management.

Some examples of how this works in practice:

- In the U.S., several development projects which cluster businesses involved in recycling around materials-recovery facilities that process municipal solid waste are under way.

- In Bangkok, a group of more than 80 tanneries has collaborated in setting up its own wastewater treatment works. Charges are made according to the production capacity of each member of the co-operative. Treatment costs are thus shared equitably and the tanneries do not see their participation as sacrificing a competitive edge.

- No industrial park has yet managed to emulate the success of a group of industries outside the small town of Kalundborg in Denmark. In this community, the outputs (wastes, water and excess energy) from several industrial processes serve as the inputs to other industrial facilities, farmers and the municipality.

■ Companies at the cutting edge

DuPont has launched a "drive towards zero emissions."[92] Procter & Gamble's "Design Manufacturing Waste Out" program aims to achieve $300 million in savings through waste and material loss reductions.[93] In its 1996 report, the company stated that it had already cut waste by 50% over five years and that by 2000 it was aiming for a further average 25% reduction of waste.

The Tokyo Electric Power Company recycles up to 90% of its own waste. By-products of the desulfurization process and coal ash are used to make cement. The company's redundant concrete poles are pulverized and used in the steel-making industry. Scrap insulation material is used to strengthen pavements.[94]

■ Supply-Chain Auditing

■ The concept

Companies that align themselves with the goals of sustainable development cannot afford to be tainted by any environmental or social misdeeds of their suppliers and contractors. Their customers will not tolerate it.

So, instead of simply auditing the environmental performance of their own operations, progressive companies are also beginning to audit the performance of their suppliers, contractors and joint-venture partners.

This is why an increasing number of corporate buyers are seeking comprehensive environmental and social information on the products or materials they purchase. This practice has become known as "supply-chain auditing."[95]

Supply-Chain Auditing implies a requirement, defined by a buyer, to provide credible and verifiable information on key environmental or social issues related to the management and production of approved suppliers.

Examples of companies adopting this approach include Fiat Auto of Italy, British Telecom, B&Q and IBM.

There are four clear business reasons for auditing the environmental performance of suppliers:

- **Compliance.** Early compliance with legislation or policy-led market incentives (such as eco-labeling) ensures that companies can take advantage of market opportunities that arise. Suppliers should be working towards such compliance.

- **Security of supply.** It is sound purchasing practice to reduce the risk that an errant supplier (one that does not read market signals on the environment or comply with the law) will be unable to supply the specified goods. Purchasers cannot afford to have their supply interrupted because it affects their ability to deliver to the next link in the chain.

- **Market opportunities.** The environmental performance of products can be a competitive issue. Companies that can supply environmentally superior products can take advantage of market opportunities.

- **Benefits versus costs.** Price was once the primary market differentiator but today quality is deemed to be equally important. Companies that invested in quality have seen long-term gains in competitiveness and profitability. Environmental quality has therefore joined the list of differentiators.

■ The "knock-on" effect of Supply-Chain Auditing

Supply-chain auditing is providing a great impetus for change among small and medium-sized companies.

Because small firms are often heavily dependent on bigger companies for their business, supply-chain auditing – which through a "knock-on effect" transmits pressure throughout the supply-chain – is an effective method for securing change. It also facilitates the transfer of knowledge and technology across borders.

Many pioneering companies that expanded the envelope in terms of improving the environmental performance of their own operations realized that real, long-term progress would ultimately depend on their ability to catalyze improvements throughout their supply or value chains.

Building on experience with **Total Quality Management** (TQM), they have been working to involve both suppliers and customers in the process of environmental improvement. Among the pioneers, is the British telecommunications giant BT, whose annual procurement spending is about £4.8 billion.[96] When companies such as these change their specifications, their suppliers naturally have to pay attention.

■ Companies at the cutting edge

One of the earliest companies to "rattle its supply-chain" was Scott, the world's leading producer of paper tissues and now part of Kimberley Clark. Companies supplying a number of markets held their breath when the news broke that Scott had dropped 10% of its suppliers. The next step was to work out ways of helping the company's pulp purchasing team make the difficult trade-offs between the environmental performance, price and quality offered by different suppliers.

The automotive sector has been one of the first to look at the possibilities offered by supply-chain management. Often, more than two-thirds of a car's parts are produced by external suppliers.

Early in 1996, Volvo's then CEO, Sören Gyll, told 500 suppliers at a major conference in Sweden that the company was launching a long-term global campaign to improve the environmental performance of its suppliers. He said environmental care would be given equal priority alongside two long-established core values: safety and quality.

Fiat Auto is reducing the number of suppliers and demanding improved quality. Its "Guidelines for Co-operation," state that "the partners accept the increasing environmental compatibility of their products and manufacturing processes as a priority, while respecting the economic and competitive balance." Our partnership with suppliers has proved valuable in creating significant improvements in quality and environmental performance.

Paolo Cantarella, Chairman, Fiat Auto

The circle of companies involved and affected is growing.

Electrical appliance manufacturer Whirlpool runs an annual Environmental Partnership Award scheme, in recognition of valued suppliers who help it improve its overall environmental performance.

Retail and distribution companies are also getting involved. The environmental report of Sainsbury's, a leading UK supermarket group, opens with a mapping of the company's supply-chain and the statement: "Sainsbury's concern for the environment covers every aspect of our supply-chain."[97] The company's UK retail business deals with more than 6,500 suppliers worldwide. Among the areas in which initiatives are already under way are: energy efficiency; integrated crop management; alternatives to animal testing; livestock rearing; and sustainable forestry.

SECTION SEVEN
Looking Ahead

If you don't think about the future you won't have one.

Anon.

Business Challenges 2020
What does the sustainable enterprise look like 20 years from now?

IN THIS FINAL SECTION of the SDX file, we 'fast-forward' to the year 2020 to see what changes have taken place in the company and in the external environment. Business will increasingly be expected to perform against a **triple bottom-line** involving economic, environmental and social needs and expectations.[98] We will therefore see that much of the debate has focused on **raising the social capital**.

A balanced policy framework between regulations and voluntary agreements may only be part of the story of the first two decades of the new century. Market and stakeholder pressures have become increasingly important. But we have moved from confrontation to co-operation.

Indeed, the predictions of the United Nations Environment Programme (UNEP) at the turn of the century — that sustainable development would be most likely to succeed (and would be achieved at the lowest overall cost to the economy) in those societies where there was the highest level of trust and other forms of 'social capital' — have proved to be prophetic.[99]

What issues will you, as a member of SDX's senior management, have to deal with in 2020?

Many issues that were emerging in the latter years of the 20th century will probably be very much still with you.

The debate about **sustainable consumption** will focus on the fast-rising needs and aspirations of the rapidly developing economies, especially China and India. Meeting these needs will demonstrate that concepts such as **Factor 10** and **eco-innovation** are essential for meeting their goals while staying within the carrying capacity of the globe.

We have seen, too, that:

▶ A society that consumes less in terms of quantity may, if that 'less' is produced, used and disposed of irresponsibly, be worse off than if it had consumed more, if that 'more' were to incorporate eco-efficient practices.

▶ Eco-innovation will continue to place a strong demand on the creativity and responsibility of individuals within a company, be they directors, managers, engineers or shop-floor workers. At every point in the value-chain, improvements can be made.

▶ Companies may now routinely ask themselves the question: 'Do our customers really need the *product* the way we have designed it, or do they need another *service*?'

You will thus still meet a lots of challenges in 2020, and the road to sustainability is long — it's a continuous process. Are you ready to join Elizabeth Chang's team and face the challenges?

Board Challenges in 2020

VIRTUAL INTER-OFFICE COMMUNICATION

SDX

To: All members of the senior management team

From: Elizabeth Chang, CEO

Date: January 7, 2020

Subject: Looking back and looking forward

There have been a number of changes at the top of SDX in recent months and several newcomers have joined the senior management team. This makes it particularly important to ensure that all team members, both old and new, are working to the same game plan.

Accordingly, I should like to reflect on some trends and developments that we shall need to discuss and arrive at a common position on at our strategy retreat in Southern France next month.

In the last 20 years, sustainable development has become a key issue in the business world. The inevitable overlap between corporate governance and sustainability issues has now entered the boardrooms of all major corporations:

▼ Many of the governance and sustainable development items on the board agenda were initially compliance-driven. As Ralph Ward noted in his book, *21st-Century Corporate Board*, "…Environmental laws put directors on the spot for assuring corporate compliance programs with penalties that can wreck a multinational corporation."[100]

▼ Today, however, voluntary partnership initiatives have become more and more widespread, as business has come to realise the competitive advantages good environmental and social management offer, and governments have adapted the policy framework accordingly.

▼ In Europe, managers are being held responsible for the performance of the company along with the whole life-cycle of the company's products. Germany and a good number of other countries have implemented tough "take-back" requirements for such sectors as packaging and auto manufacture. Negotiated agreements are, however, gaining ground in the enlarged European Union which has seen seven new countries join since the turn of the century.

▼ In the Asia-Pacific region, Japan has been among the pioneers both in environmental regulation and innovation, but other rapidly developing countries have followed suit with participatory models tailored to their own particular cultural background. China has forcefully adapted its economic growth policies to include long-term sustainability concerns.

▼ In Latin America, too, many businesses have created a competitive advantage for themselves by developing strategies that build on a practical implementation of sustainable development ideas.

Trends under way

As we enter the third decade of the 21st century, there is still a growing market for products. But their nature, and the means used to advertise and distribute them, is now very different. There has been a shift from product to services.[101]

As more governments evaluate the merits of restructuring taxes and other economic instruments in order to steer markets towards sustainable production and consumption, a differentiation has begun to emerge between the innovative company and its competitors which are entrenched in discounting the environment.[102]

By comparison with the 1990s, business today has become more involved in a debate that reaches beyond the daily sphere of work. That debate developed

▼ From efficiency to sufficiency (i.e. "enough stuff")

▼ From low-tech (e.g. lifestyle changes) to high-tech solutions (e.g. electronic highways)

▼ From incremental improvements in product design to eco-innovation (e.g. visionary products and social systems)

▼ From market-based incentives (such as government procurement policies) to the removal of environmentally harmful subsidies.

Unresolved challenges

Although much has changed this century, many of today's unresolved challenges are still those our predecessors were wrestling with in the 1990s: climate change, concern about access to freshwater, finding sustainable forms of trade to meet the need for economic growth in developing countries, and issues of social equity.

As a perusal of this complete file will show, our predecessors at SDX 20 years ago were alive to many of the issues we are now having to cope with on a daily basis. I should like to think that we can be no less prescient about the problems our successors will have to solve.

Elizabeth Chang

E.M. Chang

SustainAbility ⓒ
defining the triple bottom line of sustainable development

49-53 kensington high street
london w8 5ed
UK
tel
+44 171 937 9996
fax
+44 171 937 7447
e-mail
elkington@sustainability.co.uk

Elizabeth Chang
Chief Executive
SDX Corporation
SDX Technology Park
Cambridge, MA 10000

London, January 10, 2020

Dear Elizabeth

You asked me to reflect on the challenges you are likely to encounter once you take over the helm at SDX. I have sent you a longer note on this, drawing on the 20-plus years it has been my pleasure to interact with the company. But here are seven points drawn from that analysis.

First, SDX has now fully recovered from the turmoil of 2017–2018. The company's initial responses were badly mishandled, as you know full well, but the subsequent, ultra-transparent approach worked wonders. You have built up a good deal of credibility and trust — social capital — which should help in some of the fairly major transitions SDX now faces.

Second, it is clear that SDX's championing of the global governance agenda has both paid real dividends for the company and helped move things along. The Chinese crisis obviously helped drive us in some useful directions, but the continuing squabbles between different agencies involved in this area will make this area a political minefield for the foreseeable future. My assessment, which is spelled out in greater detail in what I have sent you, is that you should hold SDX's course on these issues — but perhaps steer some additional resources towards the South American and African initiatives.

Third, it is now 33 years — or one human generation — since the Brundtland Commission published Our Common Future. The initial pace of change was slow, but we all remember the acceleration from 1999 onwards. SDX found it hard to weather the next few years, as growing numbers of companies switched on to sustainability's 'triple bottom-line' — and some of them developed methodologies that were dramatically more powerful than those SDX had based its international platform upon. The triple bottom-line approach, I am glad to say, is now not only part of the language but also of everyday business practice. Again, SDX's leadership position has provided real business advantage.

Fourth, let me run quickly through the triple bottom-line agenda that we put together for SDX as the 21st century dawned. As you said when we last met, it really has stood the test of time. Remember that we thought of each of the three bottom-line agendas like continental plates, rubbing against each other and sometimes causing tremors or full-blown earthquakes. The 2011–14 and 2017–18 meltdowns were examples of this. In the 1999–2000 period, we focused on:

✱ The **economic–environmental 'shear zone'**, with many companies adopting eco-efficiency at the time. SDX accepted that the challenges was much wider, with environmental accounting, shadow-pricing and ecological tax reform coming up the curve.

✱ In the **social–environmental shear zone**, business was then working hard in such areas as environmental literacy and training issues, but we knew that among the new challenges would be environmental justice, environmental refugees and intergenerational equity.

✱ In the **economic–social shear zone**, some companies were already exploring the social impacts of proposed investments and projects, but bubbling under were such issues as business ethics, fair trade, human and minority rights, and stakeholder capitalism.

Fifth, most of these challenges are still with us. Decades back, Body Shop founder and CEO Anita Roddick observed that: "The triple bottom-line is becoming an imperative. Environmental and social responsibility should beat in the heart of every business leader." Well, apart from the hiccups with your infrastructure division, there is no question that all this now beats in the SDX heart. But what about the SDX brain? The capacity of corporate boards to prioritise and guide is crucial. So one of the things you will need to do urgently is to review the make-up of the SDX board, including the balance of non-executive directors, against the triple bottom-line agenda.

And, sixth, financial markets. Now that many more financial analysts understand that sound triple-bottom-line performance creates real shareholder value, SDX's stock has risen to extraordinary new levels. But this raises a real issue for you. As you begin the strategic restructuring that we all know is necessary, with thousands of people likely to lose their jobs, you will inevitably be pilloried by some NGOs and many local communities and unions. The key thing is: don't surprise them. When you take over as CEO, use the opportunity and honeymoon to announce your plans in the fullest detail to some of those most likely to be hit. Involve them in the process. Be prepared to make changes to accommodate their needs.

Seventh, as you may already know, I retire in June as Chairman of SustainAbility — although I shall continue to work on some of the programmes that are most fun! SDX, I am sure, will be one of those. SustainAbility intends to mark the transition with a virtual conference — and I would be greatly honoured if you would be one of the opening presenters.

Let's talk next week.

With best wishes,
Yours,

John Elkington
Founder and Retiring Chairman

**A Possible
Board Agenda**

SDX
Elizabeth Chang
Chief Executive Officer

To: **Board Members**
From: **Elizabeth Chang**

Notes to Agenda Item II,
Board Meeting of JANUARY 29, 2020

Why do we need to reserve an extra hour for discussing SDX's sustainability strategy?

Challenges to our global business activities arise from new sources in our market-driven world, where ad hoc social and technological innovations and high transparency require a continued dialogue with our many stakeholders.

As you know, the power of the global market is today a key driver, and the worldwide information network makes our activities fully transparent to the international NGO community. Information technology continues to help maintain a level playing field.

Today, we have less direct government involvement, although regulations are still a part of our daily business scene. But agreements are reached through mediation, as transparency is mandated. We therefore have to be clear on how we want to communicate our sustainable action strategy to our stakeholders.

The March Board Meeting must therefore address some of the most urgent issues linked to sustainability.

▼ *Item 1:* *New eco-innovation strategy*

You all know that there are enormous business consequences for having — or for not having — the most innovative eco-efficiency strategy. International standards are becoming more voluntary but, because of greater environmental awareness and transparency and the growing capacity of environmental NGOs to mount sophisticated media campaigns, we, like all our global competitors, will have to be even more aggressive in our environmental innovations. Putting it bluntly, in this highly competitive world, if you don't learn quickly and early, you're simply out of the game.

▼ *Item 2:* Briefing of the Insurance Relations Committee

The insurance industry has begun to shape our sector's investment strategy by withdrawing its support from companies with long-term environmental problems — or even from those with potential problems. National governments in conjunction with business are facilitating decision-making and are held accountable at the local level for the effects of their decisions. Self-appointed mediators are multiplying, as lawsuits come to be seen as wasteful and time-consuming.

▼ *Item 3:* The Global Partnership Award

We have just been informed that SDX will receive the Global Partnership Award for our initiative on a dispute in Peru over chlorine in the drinking water. In response to NGO pressure, the Peruvian Government reduced the amount of chlorine, and a resistant form of the cholera bug that had traveled from Bangladesh escaped, spreading cholera rapidly up the west coast of Latin America.

Thanks to our rapid initiative to create business/science/government/NGO co-operation to learn how to manage the balance between cholera, chlorine and the environment in Latin American, we managed to help control the epidemic.

▼ *Item 4:* Sustainable Development Agency
NON-RENEWABLES "RED LIST" NOTIFICATION

As you may know, the SDA consulted widely with industry prior to regulating the use of specified non-renewable inputs. At the last moment, the Agency added a number of speciality surfactants, sourced from an area that has just been designated for return to rain forest. As a direct result, two of our units have been notified by customers that they are discontinuing product lines. The knock-on effect for the surfactants division is likely to be significant: an estimated 30% hit on earnings, for a minimum of 5–6 months.

▼ *Item 5:* DESC training program

A total of 12 business units have some responsibilities under the European Commissions Duty to Educate Suppliers and Customers (DESC) provisions of the Sustainable Development Directive. Training and information programs are at last well under way. Interestingly, this could represent a major commercial opportunity. Our training teams, which have a current head-count of 29 conduct most of the training through VR programs. This represent a major investment in intellectual capital.

Is this an area for our New Business Opportunities team to take a look at? Are the DESC provisions likely to be adopted worldwide? If so, on what time-scale? Would we be best advised to build the business ourselves or spin it off?

▼ *Item 6:* International water challenges at SDX

Please see the attached memo from our advisory team.

WEBFAX MESSAGE

To: **Elizabeth Chang**
Chief Executive
SDX Corporation

From: Al Fry
Advisor on International Issues

Date: January 28, 2020

Urgent Water Challenges

You asked our team of experts to review your worldwide facilities in respect to water use and potential water conflicts. We have done so with our partners in our network, and I wish to call your attention to two new freshwater issues which could affect Corporate operations in the Middle East and Southern California

1. The SDX processing plant in Amman, Jordan, while in compliance with all national laws, is a major consumer of freshwater. In the last ten years the Government has doubled the cost of water. This cost increase was absorbed, since it still amounts to only 3% of finished product cost. The political tensions between Jordan, Syria and Israel remain tense due to the failure of the Palestinian peace process to move forward. Access to water is a key to economic development in this water-scarce region. Population continues to increase in the Amman region and competition for water is increasing. Our Jordanian partners cannot guarantee that SDX will have access to water indefinitely. Modernization of the plant is scheduled for next year.

    For an incremental capital investment of $5,000,000, SDX could move to zero water discharge. This would eliminate the need to obtain water effluent permits (an annual savings of $400,000) and eliminate any threat of future fines. Further, by recycling water inside the plant, SDX could reduce its water requirements by $1,600,000 per year. Therefore, the project would have a payback period of only two and a half years. Further, SDX could return this unused water back to the Amman authorities for redistribution to new industry or agricultural usage. Alternatively, SDX could consider relocating the plant to an area with more water and where the risk of an outbreak of hostilities were lower. SDX's Jordanian partners and the 1,500 local employees would feel betrayed by such a relocation.

2. The SDX plant in the Los Angeles basin was threatened with a temporary shutdown due to drought conditions in 1996. Closure was averted when the company managed to purchase 70 acre-feet of water from farmers in the San Joaquin valley. These farmers get low-cost water from federally subsidized irrigation schemes. The farmers made more profit from selling the water than they could from irrigating their crops and were anxious to sell. Los Angeles city officials were competing for the same water and SDX almost failed to get government approval of this emergency sale. Federal officials also hesitated to allow diversion water approved by Congress for agriculture. Several of these farmers still use outdated field flooding, primarily because the subsidized water is so cheap. They should be investing in modern drip irrigation which could reduce water needs by 80% without any loss of farm productivity. One option for SDX, would be to assist the farmers with the capital costs of newer technology and in return take permanent possession of a secure source of water from the San Joaquin valley. This would overcome all objections from Los Angeles and Federal officials. The net effect would be to reduce SDX's water charges by $1,250,000 per year to less than $100,000 (for the transportation costs). The costs for the new drip irrigation system on 160 acres of farmland is less than $1,000,000. SDX makes an immediate profit, ensures its access to freshwater and reduces inefficient irrigation practice in the San Joaquin valley.

I hope these observations will be of use to your further planning efforts.

Please transmit our agreed performance-linked consulting fee by MoneyWeb to our account at Shanghai International Bank.

Sincerely yours

Albert E. Fry

Al Fry

From the SDX Corporation Annual
Report and Accounts, 2020 . . .

LETTER FROM THE CHAIRMAN
SDX—a Sustainable Corporation

Dear Shareholder,

OVER THE LAST 20 YEARS SDX Corporation has grown in quality, profitability and reputation, and the future looks bright. We have indeed become a sustainable corporation.

Taking my voluntary retirement (as many today do when they pass 50 years of age), I thought it would be interesting to look back to see what it was that made us successful and well thought-of by so many of our stakeholders.

One reason is clearly the positive business climate we work in. Today, every government sees it as its responsibility to work with business and citizens' groups to devise a policy framework that allows realistic goals to be set and met.

Governments understood early that these goals must be based on good science and should balance ecological, economic and social objectives.

Twenty years ago, the World Business Council for Sustainable Development set out eight conditions it felt were important for success. I believe that in the past two decades those conditions have indeed proved to be vital factors behind the present health of SDX.

Let me take each one in turn:

1. freer, more open markets

TRADE IS THE LIFEBLOOD of all economies; therefore open, competitive markets have created the most opportunities for the most people. Nations with these free, open markets were the most successful in fighting poverty, and this framework provided good business conditions and the greatest opportunities for people to free themselves from the remaining poverty.

2. stable and predictable trade rules

ANOTHER REASON for the present healthy economy has been the World Trade Organization's success in limiting trade restrictions and designing environmental standards that avoided creating barriers to trade. The WTO also avoided the risk of eco-labeling schemes being distorted into trade barriers.

3. international standards

STANDARDS, such as those from the International Organization for Standardization (ISO) have shown themselves to be an effective way of providing an independent verification of quality without creating barriers to trade.

4. realistic target-setting

GOVERNMENTS now work regularly with business and other groups to set targets that recognize the realities under which business operates. These targets encourage efficiency and cost-effectiveness; and allow business flexibility of responses to meet goals set.

5. international solutions for international problems

GLOBAL ISSUES, such as the loss of biodiversity and climate change, have been handled within international frameworks, conventions, international agreements and Joint Implementation schemes. The underlying problems haven't gone away, of course, but encouraging progress has been made.

6. fast dissemination of technology

THE DEVELOPMENT and use of new technologies, and their dissemination internationally, have accelerated, thanks to suitable investment frameworks and the building-up of skills and know-how on a global basis.

7. an educated market

SUSTAINABLE DEVELOPMENT demands sustainable consumption in line with sustainable production. The first step was to make appropriate information available to consumers.

The task of providing the necessary information to allow consumers to make sensible choices would today be made still easier if costs were reflected, as much as possible, in prices and if hidden subsidies were removed.

8. economic instruments that motivate

GOVERNMENTS have used market mechanisms to encourage action. For example, the favorable treatment of investments in clean technologies — within a revenue-neutral tax shift — have speeded the introduction of those technologies.

Energy efficiency has been strongly encouraged, too, and greenhouse gas emissions per unit of output have been reduced by a system of tradable permits for emissions.

Command-and-control policies, while still a part of the general mix of policies, have proven inflexible and unduly costly for both government and business. In some cases, voluntary agreements have overcome these problems.

So, although many governments have made progress in many of these conditions, there is still a lot to be done.

I think it's fair to say that the openness and willingness for a dialogue between business, government and all other stakeholders was probably the most important driver towards a more sustainable form of development.

As I leave SDX after a 35-year career with the company and hand over to my successor, Elizabeth Chang, I do so with confidence. She was one of the young and engaged AIESEC students we picked in 1997 after she showed in the WBCSD **Sustainable Business Challenge** exam that she knew what it takes to make a company successful.

Under her chairmanship, SDX Corporation will, I know, remain a profitable and sustainable business and will be a valuable contributor to the aspirations of our society.

Piotr Kalinskij
Chairman
March 13, 2020

APPENDIX ONE

A New Vocabulary for Business

One of the best places to watch for early signals of impending market changes is the vocabulary used by successful business people.

Take the notion of the '10X' change described by Andy Grove, chairman of chip-maker Intel in his book *Only the Paranoid Survive*.[103] Grove says that the challenge in today's fast-paced markets is to find ways to survive what he calls '10X' — or tenfold — transitions that change key aspects of the market almost overnight.

Examples have included the arrival of sound in the movies industry, the transformation of the computer industry in the late 1980s and the break-up of AT&T's telephone monopoly in the US.

Among the likely '10X' factors for the 21st century is sustainable development. One early signal of the new paradigm came with a joint-authored paper in the *Harvard Business Review* by Michael Porter.[104] Its core message was that, increasingly, there are strong positive links between environmental protection, resource productivity, innovation and competitiveness.

So how do we get a sense of the underlying direction of change in the sustainable development arena — a field that is replete with its own jargon and acronyms? Here is a list of some of the words and phrases any serious student of sustainability should now be able to define:

Benchmarking. Developed in such business areas as Total Quality Management (TQM), benchmarking involves the comparison, ranking or rating of different business processes, units or companies against some standard or other. The aim: to identify ways of improving the performance of operations, systems, processes. Environmental benchmarking is a growth area.

Biodiversity. The word — a contraction of 'biological diversity' — is sometimes used as a synonym for 'life on earth'. But its specific meaning, referring to the number, variety and variability of living organisms, will be central to 21st-century values, thinking and action.

Business ecosystems. As traditional industry boundaries erode, new types of multi-industry coalitions and networks are emerging. Think of the Microsoft-Intel (or 'Wintel') business ecosystem. The real test for 21st-century businesses will be to outperform their rivals at creating the new business ecosystems needed to build and sustain a competitive, triple bottom-line (q.v.) performance.

Complementors. Those in an economy or society who supply complementary products, services or inputs to businesses or business ecosystems (q.v.). Increasingly, they can include parties once thought hostile, including competitors and campaigning groups.

Co-optition. A hybrid of co-operation and competition. A business approach that recognises that in the new economy companies may often end up working alongside, or even through, their competitors. Key players are seen to be customers, suppliers, competitors and complementors (q.v.).

Demand-side management (DSM). DSM can be applied in any industry where a product can be replaced by a service. The central principle is that a company or utility learns to provide, and have customers pay for, services (e.g. heated rooms, lighted spaces rather than kilowatt-hours or therms of gas). Often, the market needs to be provided with new price signals or other incentives.

Eco-efficiency. Involves the delivery of competitively priced goods and services that satisfy human needs and bring an improved quality of life, while progressively reducing ecological impacts and resource-intensity throughout the life-cycle, to a level at least in line with the earth's estimated carrying capacity.

Ecological footprints. The size and impact of the 'footprints' of companies, communities or individuals reflect a number of interlinked factors, among them human population numbers, consumption patterns and the technologies used. A more challenging version of the concept is 'environmental space', as developed by Friends of the Earth Netherlands/Milieudefensie.

Eco-taxes. The use of economic, and in particular fiscal, instruments for environmental protection is gaining support. Examples include charges and taxes on polluting emissions and products, tradable emission permits and deposit–refund schemes. The aim: to achieve environmental or broader sustainability policy objectives more effectively and at lower cost.

Environmental justice. In the same way that certain social groups or communities may be economically disadvantaged, so they may suffer disproportionate health, safety or environmental problems. Linked issues can surface at various types of industrial facility, from oil fields and chemical production complexes to major airports.

Environmental management system (EMS) standards. The main international EMS standard is ISO 14001. Regional EMS systems are also emerging, notably the European Union's Eco-Management and Auditing Scheme (EMAS).

Factor 4/Factor 10. Key terms used to describe resource-productivity targets over the next 50 years. Universal application of current best available technology and approaches could achieve a factor-four improvement in resource-productivity, it is argued by von Weizsäcker, Lovins and Lovins.[105] Because of population growth and increased consumption, particularly in the developing world, the developed world will also have to address the huge imbalance in the allocation of resources (the richest 20% currently use 80% of the world's resources). This means that the developed world will need to achieve at least a factor-ten improvement, as called for by the Carnoules Declaration of Schmidt-Bleek and the 'Factor 10 Club'.[106]

Full-cost accounting (FCA). Although this is an area in need of much further work, the ultimate aim is to develop accounting methods that account for all the key costs of a project or activity, not just the financial costs.

Industrial ecology. A discipline that focuses on the design, development, operation, renewal and decommissioning of industrial facilities as ecological systems, with an emphasis on the optimisation of resource efficiency.

Industry covenants. Some countries, notably the Netherlands, are encouraging particular industry sectors to agree voluntary targets — and encourage member companies towards those targets — as an alternative to new regulation. The threat of regulation, however, is always in the background.

Joint implementation (JI). JI has been proposed as a least-cost approach to cutting greenhouse gas emissions. The idea is that Annex B countries under the Framework Convention on Climate Change, which have binding commitments to cut their emissions, can invest in emission-reducing projects in countries that do not have such commitments.

Lean production. Pioneered by Toyota, this is the Japanese approach to waste management and resource efficiency. It aims to avoid the production of goods that no one wants or which fail to meet expectations, the use of processing steps that are not needed, and the non-productive transport of people or materials.

Life-cycle assessment. The overall process of assessing the environmental effect of a system, function, product or service throughout its life-cycle. Sometimes considered to include four stages: Initiation, Inventory, Impact Analysis and Improvement.

MIPS. Proposed by Professor Friedrich Schmidt-Bleek of Germany's Wuppertal Institute, the MIPS approach focuses on the 'Material Intensity Per unit Service'. The approach aims to measure the 'total material and energy throughput in mass units (like kilogrammes or tonnes) per unit good or per mass unit of good, from cradle to grave'. As the units of service clock up for a product such as a car, so the MIPS 'invested' in each unit of service supplied fall. The greater the durability of the product, within limits, the fewer the MIPS needed per unit of service.

Outrage. Perceived risk is usually a complex, volatile mix of hazard and outrage. Experts argue that companies minimise the risk of outrage when they engage stakeholders (q.v.) in the development and operation of major projects.

Precautionary principle. Policy or other action taken before the underlying science has reached absolute clarity or certainty in order to prevent 'possible' catastrophic outcomes.

Remanufacturing. Involves the recovery of equipment or products for servicing, upgrading and re-sale as working systems. Potentially offers much higher environmental returns than recycling.

Reverse logistics. The use of logistical and distribution systems to recover products or materials destined for remanufacturing or recycling.

Social capital. A measure of the ability of people to work together for common purposes in groups and organisations. A key element of social capital is the sense of trust.

Solutions campaigning. Instead of simply focusing on problems, even campaigning groups such as Greenpeace are now linking up with selected companies to develop and promote problem-solving technologies or approaches.

Stakeholders. The broadest definition of 'stakeholder' brings in anyone who affects or is affected by a company's operations. The key new perception is that companies need to expand the range of interests considered in any new development from customers, shareholders, management and employees to such people as suppliers, local communities and pressure groups.

Sustainability. There are over 100 definitions of sustainability and sustainable development, but the best known is the World Commission on Environment and Development's. This suggests that development is sustainable where it 'meets the needs of the present without compromising the ability of future generations to meet their own needs'.

Triple bottom-line. Sustainable development involves the simultaneous pursuit of economic prosperity, environmental quality and social equity. Companies aiming for sustainability need to perform not just against a single, financial bottom-line but against the triple bottom-line.

Value-impact assessment. A technique developed by Procter & Gamble to optimise the value delivered to customers and consumers, and to reduce the environmental or other impact of the manufacture, shipment, use or disposal of products.

Value migration. Market change pulls economic value from one company (or industry) and pushes it towards another. In losing control of the personal computer market, for example, it has been estimated that IBM may have lost up to $90 billion to new business ecosystems (q.v.) centred on companies such as Microsoft. The sustainability transition will also drive value migration between companies, sectors and economies.

Values shift. Over time, human and social values change. Concepts that once seemed extraordinary (for example freeing slaves and enfranchising women) are now taken for granted. New concepts such as responsible consumerism, environmental justice, and intra- and inter-generational equity, are now coming up the curve.

APPENDIX TWO

WBCSD Members 1998

- 3M Company
- ABB Asea Brown Boveri Ltd.
- Anova Holding AG
- Aracruz Celulose S.A.
- Assurances Générales de France
- AT&T
- Axel Johnson Group
- Bank Umum Nasional
- Bayer A.G.
- BG plc
- The BOC Group
- The British Petroleum Company plc
- The Broken Hill Proprietary Company Ltd
- Cargill Incorporated
- CH2M Hill
- Chemical Works Sokolov, JSC
- China Petro-Chemical Corporation (SINOPEC)
- CIMPOR
- Clifford Chance
- COGEMA
- Coors Brewing Company
- Danfoss A/S
- De Lima & Cia Ltda
- Deloitte Touche Tohmatsu International
- The Dow Chemical Company
- DuPont
- Eastman Kodak Company
- EBARA Corporation
- The Environmental Resources Management Group
- ESKOM
- Estudio Juridico Gross Brown
- FALCK Group
- Fiat Auto SpA
- Fletcher Challenge Ltd
- S.A. Garovaglio y Zorraquin
- General Motors Corporation
- Gerling-Konzern Insurances
- Glaxo Wellcome plc
- Grupo IMSA, S.A. de C.V.
- Grupo Vitro, S.A.

- Heineken N.V.
- Heinz-Wattie Limited
- Henkel KGaA
- Hitachi Ltd.
- F. Hoffmann-La Roche AG
- Hoechst Aktiengesellschaft AG
- Imperial Chemical Industries Plc
- Indonesian Forest Community
- Interface Inc.
- International Herald Tribune
- International Paper Company
- Inti Karya Persada Tehnik Pt.
- Itochu Corporation
- Johnson & Johnson
- S.C. Johnson & Son, Inc.
- Kajima Corporation
- The Kansai Electric Power Co., Inc.
- Kikkoman Corporation
- Kvaerner A.S.A.
- Lafarge
- John Laing plc
- LG Group
- March Group
- Mitsubishi Corporation
- Mitsubishi Electric Corporation
- Monsanto Company
- National Westminster Bank plc
- NEC Corporation
- Neste Oy
- Nestlé Ltd
- Nippon Telegraph & Telephone Corporation
- Nissan Motor Co., Ltd
- Noranda Inc.
- Norsk Hydro ASA
- Novartis International AG
- Novo Nordisk A/S
- Ontario Hydro
- Philips Electronics N.V.
- Pirelli SpA
- PLIVA d.d.
- PowerGen plc
- The Procter & Gamble Company
- RAO Gazprom

- Rhône-Poulenc
- Rio Doce International SA
- Rio Tinto PLC
- Saga Petroleum A.S.
- Samsung Electronics
- Scudder Kemper Investments Inc.
- Seiko Group
- Severn Trent Plc
- SGS Société Générale de Surveillance Holding S.A.
- SGS-THOMSON Microelectronics
- Shell International Ltd
- SHV Holdings N.V.
- Skanska AB
- Sonae Investimentos S.G.P.S. S.A.
- Sony Corporation
- SOPORCEL
- Statoil
- Stora
- Storebrand ASA
- Sulzer Ltd.
- Suncor Energy Inc.
- Swiss Bank Corporation
- Taiwan Cement Corporation
- Thai Farmers Bank Public Company Limited
- The Tokyo Electric Power Company Inc.
- Time Warner, Inc.
- Toyota Motor Corporation
- TransAlta Corporation
- Unilever N.V.
- UPM-Kymmene Corporation
- Vattenfall AB
- Volkswagen AG
- Waste Management International
- Westvaco Corporation
- Weyerhaeuser Company
- S.A. White Martins
- WMC Limited
- Xerox Corporation
- The Yasuda Fire & Marine Insurance Company, Ltd.
- Zurich Insurance Group

Notes

1   Stuart L. Hart, 'Beyond Greening: Strategies for a Sustainable World', *Harvard Business Review*, January/February 1997, pp. 67-76; and Joan Magretta's interview with Robert B. Shapiro, 'Growth through Global Sustainability', *Harvard Business Review*, January/February 1997, pp. 79-88.

2   Kate Fish, *Corporate Decision-Making, Sustainable Development, and Uncertainty* (DeLange Woodlands Conference, 3 March 1997).

3   World Commission on Environment and Development, *Our Common Future* (New York: Oxford University Press, 1987).

4   Philip Sarre *et al.*, *One World for One Earth: Saving the Environment* (London: The Open University/Earthscan, 1991).

5   Sarre *et al.*, *op. cit.*

6   Stephan Schmidheiny with the Business Council for Sustainable Development, *Changing Course: A Global Business Perspective on Development and the Environment* (Cambridge, MA: MIT Press, 1992).

7   D.H. Meadows, D.L. Meadows and J. Randers, *Beyond the Limits: Global Collapse or a Sustainable Future?* (London: Earthscan, 1992).

8   Claude Fussler with Peter James, *Driving Eco-Innovation: A Breakthrough Discipline for Innovation and Sustainability* (London: Pitman, 1996).

9   Michael Porter and Claas van der Linde, 'Green and Competitive: Ending the Stalemate', in Richard Welford, *Business and the Environment* (London: Earthscan, 1996); also in *Harvard Business Review*, September/October 1995, pp. 120-34.

10 Porter and van der Linde, *op. cit.*

11 Stephan Schmidheiny, Rodney Chase, Livio DeSimone with the World Business Council for Sustainable Development, *Signals of Change* (Geneva: WBCSD, 1997).

12 World Resources Institute, *The 1992 Information Please Environmental Almanac* (Boston. MA: Houghton Mifflin, 1991), p. 12.

13 United Nations Development Programme (UNDP), *Human Development Report 1994* (New York: Oxford University Press, 1994).

14 Reported in SustainAbility and the United Nations Environment Programme, *Engaging Stakeholders* (2 vols.; London: SustainAbility, 1996).

15 P. Schwartz, *The Art of the Long View: Planning for the Future in an Uncertain World* (New York: Doubleday, 1996), quoted in Fussler and James, *op. cit.*

16 Fussler and James, *op. cit.*

17 Hart, *op. cit.*

18 Schmidheiny, Chase, DeSimone with the WBCSD, *op. cit.*

19 Elizabeth Cook (ed.), *Ozone Protection in the United States: Elements of Success* (Washington, DC: World Resources Institute, November 1996).

20 Ismael Serageldin, *The Architecture of Empowerment: People, Shelter and Liveable Cities* (London: Academy Editions, 1995).

21 Peter Weber, 'Protecting Oceanic Fisheries and Jobs', in Worldwatch Institute, *State of the World 1995* (New York: W.W. Norton, 1995), pp. 21-37.

22 P. Pinstrup-Andersen, 'The Role of the Fertilizer Industry in the Future Food Production for a Growing Population' (Paper prepared for conference to celebrate the 50th anniversary of the Hydro Research Center, Porsgrunn, 1997).

23 Magretta, *op. cit.*

24 World Resources Institute, *World Resources 1988–1989* (New York: Oxford University Press, 1990), p. 94.

25 WBCSD/IUCN, *Business and Biodiversity: A Guide for the Private Sector* (Geneva: WBCSD/IUCN, 1997).

26 Stewart Boyle, 'Energy Efficiency: Time to Raise the Flag Again', in *Environment Strategy Europe* (London: Camden Publishing, 1997).

27 As quoted in Ernst Ulrich von Weizsäcker, Amory B. Lovins and L. Hunter Lovins, *Factor 4: Doubling Wealth, Halving Resource Use* (London: Earthscan, 1997).

28 Michael Brown, 'Co-Generation and Reduced Carbon Emissions', in *Environment Strategy Europe* (London: Camden Publishing, 1997).

29 Marcia D. Lowe, 'Reinventing Transport', in Worldwatch Institute, *State of the World 1994* (New York: W.W. Norton, 1994), pp. 81-98.

30   AB Volvo, *Environmental Report 1995* (Göteborg: AB Volvo, 1996).

31   ASG, *Environmental Report 1995* (Stockholm: ASG, 1996).

32   BTL, *BTL Environmental Report* (Göteborg: Bilspedition Transport & Logistics, 1996).

33   See T.E. Lovejoy, 'Lessons from a Small Country', *Washington Post*, Tuesday 22 April 1997.

34   R. Lee *et al.*, *Understanding Concerns about Joint Implementation* (Knoxville, TN: Joint Institute for Energy and Environment, October 1997).

35   Lovejoy, *op. cit.*

36   World Resources Institute, *World Resources: A Guide To The Global Environment: The Urban Environment 1996–1997* (New York: Oxford University Press, 1996), p. 247.

37   Robert Costanza *et al.*, 'The Value of the World's Ecosystem Services and Natural Capital', *Nature* 387 (15 May 1997), pp. 253-60.

38   World Resources Institute, *World Resources: A Guide To The Global Environment: People and the Environment 1994–1995* (New York: Oxford University Press, 1994), p. 153.

39   WRI, *People and the Environment 1994–1995*, p. 153.

40   WRI, *The Urban Environment 1996–1997*, pp. 230-33, 254.

41   Seventh Ibero American Conference on Education, Venezuela, 1997.

42   Ashok Khosla, summary of an article in *Development Alternatives*, September 1997, based on a speech at the World Conservation Congress in Montreal, 1997.

43   Hart, *op. cit.*

44   Hirst and Thompson, *Globalization in Question: The International Economy and Possibilities of Governance* (Cambridge, UK: Polity Press, 1996).

45   G. Ledgerwood (ed.), *Greening the Boardroom: Corporate Governance and Business Sustainability* (Sheffield, UK: Greenleaf Publishing, 1997).

46   Jonathan Charkham, *Keeping Good Company: A Study of Corporate Governance in Five Countries* (Oxford: Oxford University Press, 1995).

47   *Ibid.*

48   John Elkington, *Cannibals with Forks: The Triple Bottom Line for 21st Century Business* (Oxford: Capstone Publishing, October 1997).

49   Charkham, *op. cit.*

50   M. Flaherty, *Making the Link: Sustainable Production and Consumption* (Geneva: WBCSD, 1996).

51   Flaherty, *op. cit.*

52   US President's Council for Sustainable Development, *Final Report* (Washington, DC, 1996).

53   Organisation for Economic Co-operation and Development, *Environmental Labelling in OECD Countries* (Paris: OECD, 1991).

54   J. Elkington, J. Hailes and G. Lye, *Who Needs It? Market Implications of Sustainable Lifestyles* (London: SustainAbility, 1995).

55   Von Weizsäcker, Lovins and Lovins, *op. cit.*

56   Friedrich Schmidt-Bleek and Paul Weaver, *Factor 10: Manifesto for a Sustainable Planet* (Sheffield, UK: Greenleaf Publishing, 1998).

57   T. Levitt, 'Marketing Myopia', *Harvard Business Review* July/August 1960, pp. 45-56, quoted in Fussler and James, *op. cit.*

58   WBCSD, *Trade and Environment: A Business Perspective* (Geneva: WBCSD, 1996).

59   See National Wildlife Federation, Corporate Conservation Council and Daniel Esty, *International Trade and the Environment: Opportunities for Business and Environmental Cooperation* (Washington, DC: National Wildlife Federation, 1995).

60   United Nations Environment Programme, *UNEP Survey of Multinational Corporations* (Nairobi: UNEP, 1993).

61   Porter and van der Linde, *op. cit.*

62   WRI, *World Resources 1994–1995*, p. 5

63   M.G. Morgan, 'Risk Analysis and Management', *Scientific American* 269 (1993), pp. 32-41.

64   Elkington, *Cannibals with Forks*.

65   Schmidheiny, Chase, DeSimone with the WBCSD, *op. cit.*, p. 56.

66   Schmidheiny with the BCSD, *op. cit.*

67   The ABB Group, *Environmental Management Report 1996* (Växjö, Sweden: ABB Group, 1997).

68   Dow Europe SA, *Continuing the Responsible Care Journey 1995/96* (Horgen, Switzerland: Dow Europe SA, 1996).

69 Fussler and James, *op. cit.*

70 For more on eco-efficiency, see the WBCSD report, *Eco-Efficient Leadership* (Geneva: WBCSD, 1997); and, Livio DeSimone and Frank Popoff, *Eco-Efficiency: The Business Link to Sustainable Development* (Cambrdige, MA: MIT Press, 1997).

71 Based on a checklist proposed by Peter James, in Peter James, *Achieving Best-Practice Environmental Management* (Congleton, UK: Sustainable Business Centre, 1996), quoted in DeSimone and Popoff, *Eco-Efficiency*.

72 S. Schmidheiny and F. Zorraquin, *Financing Change: The Financial Community, Eco-Efficiency and Sustainable Development* (Cambridge, MA: MIT Press, 1996).

73 WBCSD, *Environmental Performance and Shareholder Value* (Geneva: WBCSD, 1997).

74 *Ibid.*

75 S.C. Johnson Wax, *The Environment: Our Progress Report* (Racine, WI: S.C. Johnson Wax, 1994).

76 Christopher Sheldon (ed.), *ISO 14001 and Beyond: Environmental Management Systems in the Real World* (Sheffield, UK: Greenleaf Publishing, 1997).

77 Noranda Inc., *1995 Environment, Health and Safety Report* (Toronto: Noranda Inc., 1996).

78 D. MacKenzie, *Design for the Environment* (New York: Rizzoli International Publications, 1991).

79 Xerox Corporation, *Environment, Health and Safety: Progress Report 1995* (Webster, NY: Xerox Corporation, 1996).

80 Von Weizsäcker, Lovins and Lovins, *op. cit.*

81 Schmidt-Bleek and Weaver, *op. cit.*

82 Martin Bennett and Peter James, *The Green Bottom Line: Environmental and Managerial Accounting—Current Practice and Future Trends* (Sheffield, UK: Greenleaf Publishing, 1998).

83 D. Ditz, J. Ranganathan and D. Banks, *Green Ledgers: Case Studies in Corporate Environmental Accounting* (Washington, DC: World Resources Institute, 1995).

84 Rob Gray with Jan Bebbington and Diane Walters, *Accounting for the Environment* (London: Chartered Association of Certified Accountants and Paul Chapman, 1993).

85 General Motors, *Environmental Health and Safety Report* (Detroit: General Motors, 1996).

86 Nortel/Northern Telecom, *1995 Environmental Progress Report* (Brampton, Ontario: Nortel/Northern Telecom, 1996).

87 Schmidheiny and Zorraquin, *op. cit.*

88 WBCSD, *Environmental Performance and Shareholder Value*.

89 'IRRC Survey Finds More Companies Measuring Sustainability Progress', *Business and the Environment*, December 1996, pp. 8-9.

90 SustainAbility and UNEP, *Engaging Stakeholders*.

91 LG Semicon Co. Ltd, *1995 Environmental Report* (Seoul, Korea: LG Semicon Co. Ltd, 1996).

92 DuPont, *Safety, Health and the Environment: 1996 Progress Report* (Wilmington, DE: DuPont, 1997).

93 Procter & Gamble, *P&G Environmental Progress Update 1996* (Cincinatti: Procter & Gamble, 1996).

94 For further reading on this and related subjects, we recommend the WBCSD reports: *Eco-Efficiency and Cleaner Production* (Geneva: WBCSD, April 1996) and *Sustainable Production and Consumption: A Business Perspective* (Geneva: WBCSD, May 1996).

95 Trevor Russel, *Greener Purchasing: Threats and Opportunities* (Sheffield, UK: Greenleaf Publishing, forthcoming).

96 British Telecommunications plc, *A Report on BT's Environmental Performance 1995/96* (London: British Telecommunications plc, 1996).

97 J. Sainsbury plc, *1996 Environment Report* (London: J. Sainsbury plc, 1996).

98 Elkington, *Cannibals with Forks*.

99 SustainAbility and UNEP, *Engaging Stakeholders*.

100 Ralph D. Ward, *21st-Century Corporate Board* (New York: John Wiley, 1996).

101 T. Levitt, *op. cit.*, quoted in Fussler and James, *op. cit.*

102 Fussler and James, *op. cit.*

103 Andrew S. Grove, *Only the Paranoid Survive: How to Exploit the Crisis Points that Challenge Every Company and Career* (New York: Bantam Doubleday, 1996).

104 Porter and van der Linde, *op. cit.*

105 Von Weizsäcker, Lovins and Lovins, *op. cit.*

106 Schmidt-Bleek and Weaver, *op. cit.*

Beyond the Limits: Global Collapse or a Sustainable Future? Donnella Meadows, Denis Meadows and Jørgen Randers (London: Earthscan, 1992).

Business and Biodiversity: A Guide for the Private Sector The World Business Council for Sustainable Development and The International Union for the Conservation of Nature (Geneva: WBCSD/IUCN, 1997).

Business and Climate Change: Case Studies in Greenhouse Gas Reduction The World Business Council for Sustainable Development (Geneva: WBCSD, 1997).

Business and the Environment: A Resource Guide Allison A. Pennell, Patricia E. Choi and Lawrence Moninaro for the Management Institute for Environment and Business (Washington, DC: Island Press, 1992).

By-Product Synergy: A Strategy for Sustainable Development The World Business Council for Sustainable Development (Geneva: WBCSD, 1997).

Cannibals with Forks: The Triple Bottom Line of 21st Century Business John Elkington (Oxford: Capstone, 1997).

Changing Course: A Global Perspective on Development and The Environment Stephan Schmidheiny with the Business Council for Sustainable Development (Cambridge, MA: MIT Press, 1992).

A Changing Future for Paper The World Business Council for Sustainable Development (Geneva: WBCSD, 1996).

Climate Change and the Financial Sector: The Emerging Threat—The Solar Solution Edited by Jeremy Leggett (Munich: Gerling Akademie Verlag, 1996).

Costing the Earth: The Challenges for Governments, The Opportunities for Business Frances Cairncross (London: Economist Books/Business Books, 1991).

Driving Eco-Innovation: A Breakthrough Discipline for Innovation and Sustainability Claude Fussler with Peter James (London: Pitman, 1996).

Earth in the Balance: Forging a New Common Purpose Al Gore (London: Earthscan, 1992).

The Earthscan Reader in Business and the Environment Edited by Richard Welford and Richard Starkey (London: Earthscan, 1996).

Eco-Efficiency and Cleaner Production The World Business Council for Sustainable Development (Geneva: WBCSD, 1996).

Eco-Efficiency: The Business Link to Sustainable Development Livio DeSimone and Frank Popoff with the World Business Council for Sustainable Development (Cambridge, MA: MIT Press, 1997).

Eco-Efficient Leadership for Improved Economic and Environmental Performance The World Business Council for Sustainable Development (Geneva: WBCSD, 1996).

The Ecology of Commerce: How Business Can Save the Planet Paul Hawken (London: Weidenfeld & Nicolson, 1993).

Environmental Assessment: A Business Perspective The World Business Council for Sustainable Development (Geneva: WBCSD, 1996).

Environmental Performance and Shareholder Value The World Business Council for Sustainable Development (Geneva: WBCSD, 1997).

Environmental Strategy and Sustainable Development: The Corporate Challenge for the 21st Century Richard Welford (London: Routledge, 1995).

Factor Four: Doubling Wealth, Halving Resource Use Ernst von Weiszäcker, Amory B. Lovins and L. Hunter Lovins (London: Earthscan, 1997).

Factor 10: Manifesto for a Sustainable Planet Edited by Friedrich Schmidt-Bleek and Paul Weaver (Sheffield, UK: Greenleaf Publishing, 1998).

Financing Change: The Financial Community, Eco-Efficiency and Sustainable Development S. Schmidheiny and F. Zorraquin with the World Business Council for Sustainable Development (Cambridge, MA: MIT Press, 1996).

The Green Bottom Line: Environmental Managerial Accounting—Current Practice and Future Trends Edited by Martin Bennett and Peter James (Sheffield, UK: Greenleaf Publishing, 1998).

Greener Marketing: A Responsible Approach to Business Edited by Martin Charter (Sheffield, UK: Greenleaf Publishing, 1992).

Green Inc: A Guide to Business and the Environment Frances Cairncross (London: Earthscan, 1996).

Green Ledgers: Case Studies in Corporate Environmental Accounting D. Ditz, J. Ranganathan and D. Banks (Washington, DC: World Resources Institute, 1995).

Growth and Guilt: Psychology and the Limits of Development Luigi Zoja (London: Routledge, 1995).

International Business Environmental Barometer Edited by Frank Belz and Lars Strannegård (Oslo: Cappelen Akademisk Forlag, 1997).

ISO 14001 and Beyond: Environmental Management Systems in the Real World Edited by Christopher Sheldon (Sheffield, UK: Greenleaf Publishing, 1997).

Our Common Future The World Commission on Environment and Development ('The Brundtland Report'; Oxford: Oxford University Press, 1987).

The Politics of the Real World Michael Jacobs (London: Earthscan, 1996).

Saving the Planet: How to Shape an Environmentally Sustainable Global Economy Lester R. Brown, Christopher Flavin and Sandra Postel (New York: W.W. Norton, 1991).

Signals of Change: Business Progress towards Sustainable Development The World Business Council for Sustainable Development (Geneva: WBCSD, 1997).

Silent Spring Rachel Carson (Boston, MA: Houghton Mifflin, 1962).

State of the World and Vital Signs Lester Brown *et al.* (Published annually by W.W. Norton in the US and Earthscan in the UK. The data from these Worldwatch Institute publications is available on disk; enquiries to the book publishers).

Sustainable America The President's Council on Sustainable Development (Washington, DC: US Government Printing Office, 1996).

Sustainable Industrialisation David Wallace (London: Royal Institute for International Affairs/Earthscan, 1996).

Sustainable Production and Consumption: A Business Perspective The World Business Council for Sustainable Development (Geneva: WBCSD, 1996).

Towards a Sustainable Paper Cycle The World Business Council for Sustainable Development (Geneva: WBCSD, 1996).

Trade and Environment: A Business Perspective The World Business Council for Sustainable Development (Geneva: WBCSD, 1996).

Who Needs It? Market Implications of Sustainable Lifestyles John Elkington, Julia Hailes and Geoff Lye (London: SustainAbility Ltd, 1995).